Hill Walking in Snowdonia

E.G. ROWLAND

First published by Camping and Open Air Press Ltd. 1951
Fully revised edition by Cidron Press 1958
Reprints 1961, 1964, 1967 and 1970
Revised edition by Vector Productions 1972
Revised edition by Cicerone Press 1975

Also by E. G. Rowland
THE ASCENT OF SNOWDON

Also by Cicerone Press
LLANBERIS AREA GUIDE
WINTER CLIMBS IN NORTH WALES

DEDICATED TO THE YOUTH OF BRITAIN

SBN 902 363 15 8

Indication of a route in this book
does not imply a right of way

COVER
From Tryfan (20), looking over Llyn Bochlwyd to Y Garn (17) and Elidir Fawr (18) - Photo E. Emrys Jones

Published by Cicerone Press,
16 Briarfield Road, Worsley, Manchester

Snowdon from Moel yr Ogof (7) - Photo R. B. Evans

Index

Foreword

E. G. ROWLAND derived a great deal of pleasure from this little book, both in the writing and in the subsequent travelling all over North Wales to distribute the guide. The fact that this book has now been more or less continuously in print for over twenty years is a fitting memorial to an indefatigable old climber who loved, and climbed, every one of these hills.

After Mr. Rowland's death in 1958 the publication and distribution of the guide was carried out by his close friend Jonah Jones at the Cidron Press. As a sculptor working in Tremadoc, Mr. Jones found the office work involved in distributing this guide a major distraction, but he faithfully kept the guide going through five reprints over the last fourteen years. Vector Productions produced a revised edition and now it is revised again for this edition.

Apart from a few minor revisions the text is much the same as before. It is felt that any substantial alteration would involve the loss of too much of Mr. Rowland's delightful text. Since the book was first written the number of people visiting areas Snowdonia has risen phenomenally and the resulting pressure on the hills has led to some difficulties over access in certain areas. Until the official public footpath maps are prepared it is essential that all walkers exercise the greatest of care and that they follow the suggestions made by Mr. Rowland in the Introduction.

It gives me great pleasure to be associated with this fine guide book and to be thus indirectly associated with the thousands of people who must have been, and who will be, introduced by it to the mountains of Snowdonia.

PETER CREW

"Toil he must who goes mountaineering; but out of the toil comes strength (not merely muscular energy, more than that), an awakening of all the faculties; and from the strength comes pleasure."

EDWARD WHYMPER.

Preface

A sexagenarian who orders new climbing boots—definition of an optimist by the Hon. L. S. Amery.

IN my seawashed retreat so many ramblers have asked for guidance on the best walks in our hills that I have collected the result of my own experience in this small book to reach more of them, to assist newcomers to the district and to encourage a pastime, good both for body and mind that will last, as with me, far into the " sere and yellow."

The definition which heads this page fits my case as well as the boots fitted my feet. To put it more clearly, even at the expense of modesty, all the excursions described, save one, were made while passing between the sixty-fourth and sixty-eighth milestones of my life's journey. The exception was No. 25. This was made a few days after the latter anniversary, and a solemn hornpipe was danced on the top of the Drum to celebrate the conquest of the fifty-third and final peak. How ever, it should be added that I had a very good grounding in these hills in younger days, before the fates took me far from them.

As the toils of life were over, I was free to select suitable days for the outings and they were, in the main, fair weather trips. But now and then rain, mist, gales, snow and ice were encountered. Still nightfall always saw a safe ending to every journey, and, on most of them, horizons were wide under blue skies, the turf was elastic and the shining waters " marched in music to the sea."

I would add a word directed especially to my young friends to whom I dedicate this book. As my rambling days are ending, I hand it to you in the hope that it will increase the happiness of your wanderings.

How good it is to find, that year by year, more and more of you come tramping, climbing and camping in Snowdonia. You cannot spend your spare time with more profit. I would ask you to mix with the courage and effort that you bring to the hills, a dash of discretion and good manners, so that your pleasures are not marred by hurt to yourselves nor trouble to other people. May good fortune go with you in all your ways. Make them as high as you can.

Llys Owen, Criccieth, 1951. E. G. ROWLAND.

Mountains in Snowdonia

Qualification: A distinct Peak of 2000 feet or over
(Arranged in order of altitude)
(See diagrams inside the covers for position of the peaks)

No.	Name	Height in feet	Height in Metres	Section	No. of Walk
1.	Snowdon	3561	1085	B.	1 to 6
2.	Crib y Ddysgl	3493	1065	B.	6
3.	Carnedd Llywelyn	3485	1062	D.	23
4.	Carnedd Dafydd	3427	1044	D.	23
5.	Glyder Fawr	3279	999	C.	16
6.	Glyder Fach	3262	994	C.	16
7.	Penyrolewen	3211	979	D.	23
8.	Foel Grach	3196	974	D.	24
9.	Yr Elen	3152	961	D.	23
10.	Y Garn	3104	946	C.	17
11.	Foel Fras	3092	942	D.	24
12.	Elidir Fawr	3030	924	C.	18
13.	Crib Goch	3023	921	B.	6
14.	Tryfan	3010	917	C.	20
15.	Y Lliwedd	2947	898	B.	6
16.	Yr Aryg	2876	877	D.	24
17.	Moel Siabod	2860	872	E.	19
18.	Llwytmor	2750	838	D.	24
19.	Pen yr Helgi-du	2733	833	D.	22
20.	Foel Goch	2727	831	C.	17
21.	Carnedd y Filiast	2695	821	C.	18
22.	Mynydd Perfedd	2665	812	C.	18
23.	Nameless (near Glyders)	2636	803	C.	16
24.	Pen Llithrig-y-wrach	2622	799	D.	22
25.	Bera Mawr	2588	789	D.	24
26.	Moel Hebog	2566	782	A.	7
27.	Elidir Fach	2565	782	C.	18
28.	Drum	2529	771	D.	25
29.	Moelwyn Mawr	2527	770	E.	14
30.	Gallt yr Ogof	2499	762	C.	16
31.	Yr Aran	2451	747	B.	11
32.	Craig Cwm Silyn	2408	734	A.	8

33.	Craig Eigiau	2390	728	D.	25
34.	Moel Eilio	2383	726	B.	10
35.	Moelwyn Bach	2334	712	E.	14
36.	Trum y Ddysgl	2329	710	A.	8
37.	Garnedd Goch	2301	701	A.	8
38.	Mynydd Mawr	2291	698	A.	9
39.	Allt Fawr	2287	697	E.	15
40.	Mynydd Drws-y-coed and Y Garn	2286	697	A.	8
41.	Cnicht	2265	690	E.	13
42.	Creigiau Gleision	2214	675	D.	21
43.	Moel Cynghorion	2207	672	B.	10
44.	Moel Druman	2152	656	E.	15
45.	Mynydd Tal-y-mignedd	2148	655	A.	8
46.	Moel yr Hydd	2124	647	E.	14
47.	Foel Gron	2100	640	B.	10
48.	Moel Lefn	2094	638	A.	7
49.	Pen y Castell	2035	620	D.	25
50.	Gallt y Wenallt	2032	619	B.	12
51.	Moel yr Ogof	2020	616	A.	7
52.	Gyrn Wigau	2019	615	D.	24
53.	Tal y Fan	2001	610	D.	26

NOTES

2. This name on the O.S. map refers to the crest up to it, the summit where the O.S. cement block is situated being Carnedd Ugain (The Cairn of Twenty).

23. This is sometimes called Moel-y-Caseg (Mare's Hill), from the small lake at its west side.

33. Name not on O.S. map.

40. The height on O.S. map is that of Y Garn, a spur of the main peak.

51. Name not on O.S. map.

CHAPTER ONE

Introducing Snowdonia

"Perhaps in the whole world there is no region more picturesquely beautiful than Snowdon, a region of mountains, lakes, cataracts and groves, in which nature shows herself in her most grand and beautiful forms."

GEORGE BORROW

FOR over two centuries a compact area in North Wales has been called Snowdonia. It forms the northern half of the Snowdonia National Park, contains the highest mountain south of the Border and over 50 peaks exceeding 2,000 feet in height. It is mainly a wild and rugged region, interspersed with beautiful valleys. It has long been a favoured holiday centre for those who wish to escape from the stresses of modern urban life to lonely places. Of late this popularity has greatly increased.

There is an extensive literature dealing with the district but it is felt that a gap may be filled by this small volume, intended to help those who delight to wander on its high places. It sets out a detailed account of tested routes up and down every peak in the area that exceeds 2,000 feet, with alternatives and variations. There are also a few notes on other excursions, some general information and chapters on the countryside and Countryside Societies.

While the main object of this book is to encourage beginners, and especially young ones, to come to these hills for a sport that will give them life-long pleasure, more practised walkers should find some new routes of interest to them. Naturally much is left to the reader's imagination. He can adapt the excursions to his personal taste, physical ability and time available. The hard-boiled rock climber is not catered for. He usually belongs to a Climbing Club and has an extensive library devoted to his more hazardous pastime.

Obviously there are many omissions. These uplands are spacious and it would take a lifetime to explore them completely. As most ramblers like a definite object on their outings, summit cairns are the climax to most of the trips. If the routes described are followed, goals should be reached with less effort and more profit than otherwise. Due apologies are tendered for the inevitable overlapping in the details of some of the excursions.

The average person with a clear head and reasonable strong leg muscles should have no trouble on any of these walks. Here and there the easy scrambling indicated adds a little zest to the outings.

Few sports excel the age old pastime of walking in the countryside. When it is enjoyed amid the finest surroundings in Great Britain, it is at its best. But conditions on the uplands differ somewhat from those lower down and therefore a few general remarks for the benefit of newcomers must preface the main part of this book.

Until our National Parks are more fully established and the legislation relating to footpaths completed, the proviso printed about this on Ordnance Survey maps must hold good here, While every effort has been made to ensure accuracy, no responsibility can be assumed as to the right of way over any of the paths described. In practice it will be found that existing roads, tracks and footpaths can be used and that the farming fraternity will not hinder the wayfarer, but often give valuable help as long as he observes the golden rules for ramblers: leave all gates as you find them, avoid all standing crops, keep dogs under control, repair any accidental damage done to walls, hedges or fences, and leave no litter. In the upper reaches there is much freedom.

On the favoured hills—Snowdon and a few others, and on the routes to popular cliff climbs—paths, more or less clear, will be found or small cairns may mark the direct way. Elsewhere one's own route must be worked out. When this is done successfully the pleasure of the trip is enhanced.

On some lower ground and even high up, bogs are frequent. Though seldom dangerous, they should be avoided for the sake of dry feet. They can usually be seen from a distance, distinguished by a growth of reeds. If a section must be crossed, nip over quickly by hopping from tuft to tuft. But you must by-pass the few soft and deep morasses, often covered by bright emerald moss.

In the summer time, wading through bracken is toilsome and at all times heather makes for hard slogging. Patches of these can often be avoided, but sometimes sheep tracks lead through them. These tracks can at times be taken for paths, though they seldom go far in the right direction. Do not trust bracken for hand-holds on steep slopes, but live heather will usually support you owing to its deep roots. Perhaps the worst going is over bracken and heather covering irregular stones, but big scree at a steep angle runs this close.

You should cross any of the high stone walls that may bar your progress with great care and without profanity. They were not built to obstruct the tourist. Some of them date from the time of the Enclosures and many are boundary fences to keep in check the native sheep that, unlike their more placid Southdown relatives, are filled with fierce Celtic blood and can negotiate anything less than a five-foot wall or a five-barred gate with the greatest of ease.

In many cases grass slopes lead through to the top. Even when they are steep they need care only when very wet or very dry. You can often mount at the side of small cliffs that provide steadying handholds. But your hands will seldom be wanted, except on such ascents as Tryfan, the Bristly Ridge and the Crib Goch crest. Test your hand grips well before putting your full weight on them, and do not be afraid of leaning well out from the hill to improve your balance.

On approaching any ascent it is as well to pick out a suitable line of attack from a distance, noting the stretches of grass that lead upwards through heather or bracken and any steep rock faces to be avoided. The straight way up is not always the quickest. Note any landmarks such as trees, walls or rocks near the chosen route, because the actual summit may be lost to sight as you advance. Coming down a strange slope it is not easy to avoid steep cliffs, so go slowly, always retaining a line of retreat. Do not jump from ledge to ledge, hoping for the best.

The weather up here has a bad reputation that it does not always deserve. On most days some excursion can be made. Indeed, in showery weather there are often cloud effects of great beauty and the atmosphere has a pellucid clearness when the rain ceases. Should this happen wide distant views open up, unknown in hot, hazy periods. When it does rain, it may be a gentle fall merging into mist above, or a fierce downpour cutting horizontally across the wilds, rendering the stoutest raincoat more of a protest than a protection. The watercourses will sing with a deeper note and the bogs be more spongelike than ever, as they sink under your feet. It does not do much harm to get soaked once in a way and there is some satisfaction in battling with the elements and completing a climb in spite of them. The hotel on Snowdon often has its dripping walkers mingling with those who have ascended dryshod in the train. Both have the same negative view on these occasions.

Greater danger lurks in the mists when they roll across the heights. Do not press on in unknown or pathless high country when they swirl around; the attempt may land you in for a long period of exposure, with a chance of a sudden drop of a few hundred feet. If you have noted a few landmarks on the way up, it should not be difficult to retrace your steps, aided by a map and compass. If there is any wind note its direction and always take a compass bearing before the landscape is obscured. Study the map for any streams that may help you down if the contour lines are well spaced, but if the contours are close together you may be landed in a series of waterfalls, with edges too steep to negotiate.

The wind, too, a friend when cooling breezes ease the early slogging up the lower slopes, can be an enemy if it rages across an exposed ridge that you have to tackle. Deal with it by keeping to leeward of the crest, if this is not too steep, or by changing direction to a course that keeps it in your back. Most of the accidents to walkers are due to inexperience or the neglect of obvious precautions.

While these minor troubles are mentioned, they need not loom too heavily and, if any arise, they are soon forgotten in the joys of long days on the heights, the entrancing views, the radiant air that stimulates a noble appetite, and the happy walk homeward in the sunset glow, so often a glorious climax to days in the sun.

The majority of visitors come here in the three summer months and cause not a little congestion in the resorts. It is to be hoped that the staggering of holidays will ultimately extend the season, since there is no better time for walking than in the spring and autumn. The weather is usually kinder and the undergrowth less troublesome. The countryside is crowned with beauty, either by the fresh green of promise, or the mellow tints of another year's achievement.

If you can find a few days in mid-winter, a visit to these hills will give you a great reward. Daylight is shorter and plans must conform to this, but the lower temperatures allow of faster progress. Snow is usually found on the heights and sometimes at lower levels. Strange, glistening effects alter familiar landscapes and the hills seem vastly higher under their pure white coating. You leave footprints across untouched drifts, find sheets of ice on the lakes and wander among ghostly peaks in intense solitude. No medico can prescribe a tonic equal to these semi-alpine wanderings.

The mild cautions already given apply with greater force to winter conditions. The rocks are often ice coated and drifts and cornices of snow add dangers that need extra care. Among crags and on steep slopes an ice axe is essential, but know how to use it before slinging it over your shoulder. It is as well to stick to well known tracks, to have a companion and to retreat at once should a mist descend or a gale blow up.

To enjoy these walks, go slowly and steadily in the early stages. As a rule they are the stiffest part of the day's work and you do not want to arrive on the skyline hot and bothered. Leaders of parties must remember the naval axiom that the speed of a fleet is that of the slowest vessel, and not force the pace so as to distress the weaklings. A party should keep well together, especially in bad weather.

As to equipment, there are few absolute necessities, but among them are the 1:50,000 Ordnance Survey map of the area and a pocket compass. All the excursions, with the exception of one of the lower walks in Chapter VII and some outliers described in Chapter VIII, are covered by Sheet No. 115, "Caernarvon and Bangor" of the new 1:50,000 map. It may be noted that many of the paths shown on it, particularly in the higher regions, are not always easily traced.

Your feet will do most of the work and must be looked after. Boots should be stout, waterproof and, above all, comfortable. The soles should be of the Vibram or Commando type, with deep cleats. Smooth soles, Tuf boots and the like are dangerous and highly unsuitable. Socks should be thick and if there is room in your boots for two pairs, so much the better. New boots must be broken in slowly, otherwise you are almost sure to end up with painful blisters.

Clothing is very much up to the individual, his budget and the conditions of the day. An absolute essential is a wind and waterproof anorak. The lightest and cheapest are made from special nylon cloth, though these tear rather easily. Over-trousers of the same material are useful for heavy rain. A warm pullover should be taken, even on the warmest of days—it is usually much cooler higher up. In cold weather a woollen cap or balaclava and gloves make a vast difference to comfort. Woollen trousers or, preferably, breeches are best. Shorts are totally unsuitable on their own. Even in summer, always take some spare clothing to put on when resting. In winter this is a vital necessity. If in doubt, do not be afraid to ask for advice.

Except for short walks a rucksack is needed. The best for the purpose are those of light canvas cloth without the needless weight of a frame. It should hold the refreshments (not forgetting a reserve in case of unexpected delays), spare clothing, a small first aid outfit and any oddments you fancy. If going alone for long trips, include an electric torch and a whistle. Binoculars are useful both for route finding and for enjoying the scenery and a sharp knife has many uses. A stick helps in prodding bogs but gets in the way if you enjoy a little scrambling. An ice axe, as mentioned above, is only needed when high-level winter work is attempted.

The length of this list need not alarm you. It gives hints to cover all normal conditions and can be modified to suit individual tastes. As in most things, trial and error will soon show you how to sally forth, ready for all reasonable eventualities.

SPECIAL NOTE

It is emphasised that the one-inch or the new 1:50,000 map of the area to be covered should be carried on all extended expeditions. All the excursions given in the text were made with its assistance and the spelling throughout follows it.

The area of the sketch maps on the insides of the covers is covered by Sheet No. 115 of the recent 1:50,000 Ordnance Survey Series. It is also shown in much greater detail on 12 sheets of the 1:25,000 series (2½"). Until Public Rights of Way are indicated on the Caernarvonshire section of the O.S. map, a useful source of information is the 1:25,000 map published by West Col Productions. All of these maps are available locally.

"The hills are beautiful. They are beautiful in line and form and colour; they are beautiful in purity, in their simplicity and in their freedom; they bring repose, contentment and good health."

F. S. SMYTHE

"They (the Alps) have been to me the well springs of life and joy. They have given me royal pictures and memories that can never fade. They have made me feel in all my fibre the blessedness of perfect manhood, causing mind and soul and body to work together with a harmony and strength unqualified by infirmity or ennui."

JOHN TYNDALL

CHAPTER TWO

The field to conquer

"There is no corner of Europe that I know . . . which so moves me with the awe and majesty of great things as does this mass of the northern Welsh mountains, seen from this corner of their silent sea."

HILAIRE BELLOC

SNOWDONIA, a name with some warrant from antiquity, covers some three hundred square miles of mainly mountainous country, centred on Snowdon itself. Roughly it is bounded by a line running from Conway to Caernarvon, thence southward to Criccieth, east to Llan Ffestiniog and then north again to Conway.

As will be seen from the map on the inside cover its shape is a reversed capital L with its ends joined by a curved line. From the sea outside this line, three valleys run into the hills, rise over watersheds and then go down to meet a cross valley coming north-east from the Irish Sea. This cross valley cuts off the angle in the corner of the letter L. Thus there are five areas in all, four on the sides of the three valleys and a fifth in the corner. For convenience of reference they have been marked A, B, C, D and E in the diagram.

All four valleys contain main roads. They are:

(1) the Caernarvon-Beddgelert road;
(2) the Llanberis Pass from Caernarvon to Pen-y-gwryd;
(3) the Nant Ffrancon Pass from Bethesda to Capel Curig; and
(4) the Portmadoc-Betws-y-coed road, passing through the Vales of Glaslyn and Nant Gwynant and going on via Capel Curig.

The junctions of the three valleys with the cross one are at Beddgelert, Pen-y-gwryd and Capel Curig, while the crests of the watersheds are at Rhyd-ddu, Pen-y-pass and Llyn Ogwen.

As might be expected, the junctions and crests are centres of hill walking and are used a good deal by visitors. Llanberis, which to some extent takes the place of bleak Pen-y-pass, must be added to the list. In addition there are many places on the edge of the area where ramblers can share their time between the hills, the sea and the milder beauties of lower regions. These include the many resorts along the north coast, with Criccieth, Portmadoc, Maentwrog, Ffestiniog, Betws-y-coed, Llanwrst and Trefriw on the other sides. From any of these outer places the hills can be reached by car at some point within an hour.

That excellent standard work, *The Mountains of Snowdonia*, lists 49 peaks that top 2,000 feet and of these 14 exceed 3,000 feet. The list on pages 6 and 7 has them all, with a few additions that seemed to merit inclusion. To qualify there must be a crest, distinct from high land leading up to some other peak. Among so many giants and satellites, there is ample room for exploration.

The walks described give routes to the summits of all the listed peaks, either singly or in combination with others. Every one has been tested by actual trial and enough detailed directions are given to ensure that the newcomer keeps on a line that will give a good ascent and a safe return from the top. Every attempt has been made to afford variety. In some cases a well-recognised route to the cairn has been given and alternative descents suggested; in others a circular expedition is outlined. This has been done to suit the two main classes of walkers. The first use cars or cycles to reach a starting place and can take off from any road point; the second use rail or bus and can make any desired traverses. The former are tied to a base and the latter are hampered by time tables. It is an imperfect world. Luckily the district has good main roads and is served with a reasonable system of public transport (except on Sundays).

As most people spend their holidays in one place, the walks are cut up into daily rations, with a few half-day portions. The freer minority, who go on walking tours and rove from one bed to another, can combine the trips to suit their itinerary and should find the details of particular ascents useful.

Figures for times and distances are apt to be misleading and therefore are seldom given. A mile upward in the rough is often equal to two on a hill path or three on a main road. It is said that it takes an hour to climb 1,000 feet, but this can often be beaten without undue effort. You can go down an hour's climb in an easy 40 minutes.

The diagram on the inside cover shows the whole ground in miniature. It shows the peaks under numbers, the main roads and the Sections A to E. The Excursions, after dealing with the Snowdon Massif, give the walks from each junction and watershed. They are numbered to allow for cross references. Some lower walks and a few outside peaks are described. The word "climb" is not used in the technical sense employed by cragsmen in their specialised hobby.

In all cases R=Right and L=Left. The figures in brackets indicate feet above sea level.

CHAPTER THREE

THE EXCURSIONS

The Snowdon Massif

"A vast mist enveloped the whole circuit of the mountain. The prospect down was horrible. It gave an idea of numbers of abysses, concealed by a thick smoke, furiously circulating about us. Very often a gust of wind formed an opening in the clouds, which gave a fine and distinct vista of lake and valley." (Summit of Snowdon).

THOMAS PENNANT

SNOWDON (3561), the tallest giant and the Mecca of all walkers on their first visit to North Wales, deserves the pride of place. Few days pass without someone standing on the summit cairn and, in the summer season and at Bank Holiday times, it can be positively congested. It is worth noting that on a recent sunny Christmas Day well over 100 ramblers climbed it. They were rewarded with a grand view, and a wonderful after-glow as the red sun set.

Of the five main routes up the mountain, three can be started from or near Beddgelert, one from Pen-y-pass at the top of the Llanberis Pass and the fifth from Llanberis itself.

1. THE RHYD-DDU PATH

There are two starting points for this route both on the Beddgelert-Caernarvon road. (1) Leave the main road R at Pitt's Head by a farm road to Ffridd-uchaf, marked by a bunch of conifers. Leaving the farm L take a path partly beside a wall till the by-road from Rhyd-ddu is reached. (2) From the new parking ground just short of Rhyd-ddu village, follow an old quarry track for a mile. When the faint grass path from Ffridd-uchaf is met R, leave the track through a narrow gate L. Here the ways unite. Go through a wall running up the shoulder of the hill above. Pass a rocky mound, near which you may trace the ruins of a hut, where refreshments could be had in the very old days. Soon you reach a third wall. The marked path goes through this for a curve round the contour line, but time can be saved by ascending by the side of the wall, until you reach the rim of the wonderful Cwm Clogwyn.

At this point many a young climber has had his first view of the impressive desolation of most of the high Welsh valleys. Upwards along the edge, Llechog, the fairly steep path bears traces of generations of climbers, who have been glad to turn along the more level stretch on the face of Bwlch Main (3,000). Soon the Saddle is reached, with mighty cwms on either side, and the last lap leads up along a jagged ridge with one or two grass patches until a concrete building looms into sight and the task is ended by a scramble up the huge summit cairn. This is said to have been built by Ordnance engineers, and was once disfigured by wooden shanties now removed.

By the way, the Saddle and upper part have been given a bad name by people who suffer from vertigo, but actually the path is as safe as a highway to most walkers. This route via Fridd-uchaf is roughly that used by the Beddgelert guides who used to race up and down for a small prize in the good old days. That these Highland Gatherings are no longer held in Wales is a loss to local life in the hills.

Having reached your first peak you must "view the landscape o'er." Many able pens have described the panorama and a quotation from George Borrow's *Wild Wales* is as good as any:

"There we stood enjoying a scene inexpressly grand, comprehending a considerable part of the mainland of Wales, the whole of Anglesey, a faint glimpse of part of Cumberland, the Irish Channel and what might be either a misty creation or the shadow of the hills of Ireland. Peaks and pinnacles and huge moels stood up here and there, about us and below us, partly in glorious light, partly in deep shades . . . But of all the objects that we saw, those that filled us with admiration and delight were numerous lakes and lagoons, which, like sheets of ice or polished silver, lay reflecting the rays of the sun in the deep valleys at our feet."

It is of interest to note that, while long usage has made Snowdon the name of the peak, the Welsh title is Y Wyddfa, meaning the tomb or barrow, from a legend that a giant was buried there. The word Eryri, still sometimes used, is shortened from "Creigiau Eryri" or the rocks of the eagles, a term applying to the whole region round the summit. Today no eagles fly there.

2. THE LLANBERIS PATH

Turning to the other routes up Snowdon, little need be said of the long trudge up from Llanberis. The path is obvious throughout. It starts near the Mountain Railway Station and twists and turns a bit near the track most of the way. There are some pleasing features. The train is available if you weary and refreshments can be had at the Halfway House, kept by the same family for over seventy years. Moreover, the views increase in beauty to a climax. On the L there is a stupendous vista of Llanberis Pass at Clogwyn Station, while opposite the cliffs of Clogwyn Du'r Arddu show the hardest rock climbs south of the Border. The ascent can be more strenuous, if you turn L up the grass slope at Hebron Station, and proceed to Clogwyn along the varied skyline.

If you are returning to Llanberis, do so over the top of Crib-y-Ddysgl (3,493), (6), about half-a-mile to the north, surmounted by an Ordnance column marking Snowdon's nearest rival. This will add another peak to your bag and furnish an amusing descent. From the column, keep the edge of the cliffs on your R, leaving the crest when your nerve is equal to the task of scrambling down into the lost valley of Cwm Glas (VII.ii.e), with its two tarns, which should be kept well to the R. The cwm is the haunt of the botanist and rock climber and you can do a little exploration to find the easiest way down to the main road in Llanberis Pass. This should be reached near Beudy-Mawr. If lucky, you may find a bus to Llanberis on your homeward way.

3. THE SNOWDON RANGER PATH

This starts behind the Youth Hostel on the peaceful shore of Llyn Cwellyn, with the main Caernarvon-Rhydd-ddu road beside it. Pass a farmhouse and observe the notice by keeping to the zigzags till the pasture land is left behind, at the corner of two stone walls. Circle round the base of Cwm Clogwyn, to avoid the boggy land that is rather prevalent hereabouts, leaving the lake R to reach a steeper and more rocky path. After this you will toil up the ridge of Clogwyn Du'r arddu. Keep well to the L of the path to look down the climbers' cliffs from above (2). On the R, Cwm Clogwyn sweeps up to the summit behind three small tarns. Soon you reach a plateau and slant across to the railway line to turn R for the last short lap.

This path seems to have been the earliest used to reach the summit, in fact Pennant himself ascended by it. The Youth Hostel, formerly an inn, then a religious house, was again a hotel before being taken over for its present use. It it named after the first professional guide in these parts. The route is as interesting as the Rhyd-ddu Path and the two can be combined easily, since the starting points are only a mile-and-a-half apart and there is a bus service between them.

4. THE SIR EDWARD WATKIN PATH

This path dates back to September, 1892, when it was opened to commemorate a visit by Gladstone, who, at the age

Snowdon from the Watkin Path (4) - Photo E. Emrys Jones

of 84, walked up to a rock a thousand feet above sea level to address the Welsh nation on freedom for small states. Faded photographs show that seldom have so many people gathered together on the slopes of Snowdon.

Leave Beddgelert by the Capel Curig road and, half-a-mile beyond Llyn Dinas, take a by-road L, through a gate leading upwards by a white chalet and on to a series of very fine waterfalls. For parking there is a new car park just beyond the start, on the main road. At the top of the falls is a wooden bridge, near a house ruined by Commandos training for D-Day. Traces of their realistic mimic warfare can still be seen in and around the building. Hard by is the rock whence Gladstone delivered his oration, duly inscribed with details in two languages.

Pass on up the cwm to a deserted slate quarry, but turn R at the near end of the roofless huts and proceed up a tiring shaly path that twists and turns a bit till the ridge is reached. Step over the far edge of this R and again your toil is amply rewarded. The view of Llyn Llydaw below and the stretch of country to the east is superb, and northwards the grim pinnacles of Crib Goch shut out the Llanberis Pass and lead the eye L to the finest close-up of Snowdon, while on the R the cliffs of Y Lliwedd look very steep indeed. Passing along the ridge there seems a good deal yet to be done. From the summit to Llyn Glaslyn below is 1,500 feet and you are only a short way up its edge. Unluckily the old path is nearly rubbed out by weathering, but if a slant is taken L, the Rhyd-ddu Path (1) will be reached near the summit. Turn R on reaching the cairn that marks the junction. If returning the same way, try the Aran side of the Cwm, rising over the crest of Bwlch Main L from the Rhyd-ddu Path and, when the slope eases, make for the upper slate works below you.

5. THE PYG TRACK (P.Y.G. TRACK)

It is said that this route gets its name because it was made by early visitors to Pen-y-gwryd Hotel. It is also called the Capel Curig path, but it is a far cry to that village. The main road is left at Pen-y-pass on the top of Llanberis Pass (1,169), so that the actual climb is shorter, though somewhat steeper, than the others. Take the rough path behind the stone enclosure opposite the hostel. It is well worn and clearly marked by cairns as it skirts the northern side of the foothills, with good views of the Pass of Llanberis and the stern Glyders on the other side of it.

After a mile of dodging wet places and spotting cairns,

Snowdon from Llyn Llydaw (5) - Photo E. Emrys Jones

bear L to a col known as Bwlch Moch to obtain a grand view of Llyn Llydaw and a sheer side of Snowdon, rising over the gloomiest cwm in Wales. The rocky route to the top of Crib Goch (6) is just behind and you leave it l. for a path under its crest. After a more or less level mile you reach an old copper mine. Do not follow the path to it—that has misled many walkers—but rise R of it to start up the famous Zigzags. These carry you steeply to the skyline above. The lake below L is Llyn Glaslyn, source of the river of that name, and it is surely the most sunless tarn of them all. The path here may be missed in thick weather. In that case keep well R to miss the steep cliffs L. At the top of the ridge keep L and find the railway track to finish the ascent.

To vary the descent, turn down R to Llyn Glaslyn from the copper mine and return along the shores of the two lakes ending by the by-road to Pen-y-pass (6).

It may be noted that yet another way up is by the alternative descent given in (2) through Cwm Glas.

Several fine traverses offer themselves. Perhaps the best are: Up by (5) and down by (2) and, Up by (4) and down by (1) or (3).

6. THE HORSESHOE WALK: CRIB GOCH, CRIB Y DDYSGL, SNOWDON AND Y LLIWEDD

Before leaving the popular centre of the district, the Horseshoe Walk must be described. It is considered the finest ridge walk in Great Britain, but it is strenuous and should only be attempted by the fit in clear mild weather. In mist and rain it is a thankless grind and, in the snow and ice of winter expert climbing knowledge and equipment are essential. Under the best circumstances some scrambling is needed and you must be prepared for about eight miles of switch-backing over the highest parts of Wales.

The start is usually made from Pen-y-pass, taking Crib Goch (3,023) first. This is the route now followed, as the reverse is less interesting. Go up the Pyg Track (5) as far as Bwlch Moch, where the rocky face of the first peak rises just behind you. The grassy hollow must be left and its eastern arête tackled. It is rather steep, with an exposed point or two, and furnishes the first test of your powers. If it is too troublesome, retrace your steps to the Bwlch and reach the top of Snowdon by the Zigzags (5) continuing the round from that point, whence there is little trouble.

However, the first scramble will probably encourage you to proceed to the summit ridge of Crib Goch. The proper way is well defined. On many rocks you will see whitish marks made by the thousands of nailed boots that have preceded yours. These scratches are a great comfort on all the more frequented rock walls. They tell you that you have not strayed from normal routes and indicate the best way to proceed.

When you top the ridge, you have a glorified edition of the Bwlch Moch panorama, from one of the finest view-points of all. The prospect can be found in most of the photographic books, from Abraham's to Poucher's. It includes all the task ahead, the ridge before you, the path rising up to Crib y Ddysgl, the massive outline of Snowdon, the long sweep down and shorter rise to the twin Lliwedds and finally the slopes of Llyn Llydaw. If a late start indicates that lunch should be taken at this early stage, you may be able to share it with the sea-gulls that are so often as tame in this remote spot as on London Bridge.

The knife edge ahead is the stiffest part of the round. In the old textbooks it was classified as the easiest rock climb, though the modern rubber-soled gymnasts would scorn this description. It is narrow with sharp drops on either side and the top must be adhered to. Luckily the footholds are on the less steep side. Most folks use their hands freely in crossing it and look out for the boot marks just mentioned so that they can step on them while holding on to the actual top. When near the end, drop down a bit L to circumvent the most famous Pinnacle, which can only be scaled by a little airy rock work.

A. P. Abraham in his *Beautiful North Wales* quotes an entry in a hotel visitors' book: "So-and-So ascended the Crazy Pinnacle in five-and-a-half minutes and found the rocks very easy." Below was another entry: "Our party *descended* the Crazy Pinnacle in five-and-a-half *seconds* and found the rocks very hard."

After clearing the rocks you will drop down to the grass of Bwlch Goch and relax a little on this pleasant saddle. It forms the crest of a good walk from Llanberis Pass through Cwm Glas (2) (VII.ii.e) and down to Llyn Glaslyn (5), nestling right under Snowdon.

The next stage is the ascent of Carnedd Ugain, usually called Crib y Ddysgl (3,493) (2). The path is a succession of rocky twists and small grass saddles. After the second grass patch, it is very easy to bear too much to the L and find yourself just over the Zigzags (5). This means a stiff pull up to regain the crest. Avoid this by keeping R up some steep rocks at the doubtful point. Walkers seem to have tried a variety of routes up this imposing half mile, but ere long you will reach the Ordnance column on the top of Crib y Ddysgl (2). Thence it is plain sailing down to the railway track and up to the summit of Snowdon. You have now earned your lunch and it is hoped that the state of the atmosphere will allow you to see Ireland.

Rested and refreshed, the easier half of the round can now be undertaken more lightly. It is remarkable how the higher reaches tend to yield unsuspected stores of energy that may at times deceive the walker into tasks a bit beyond his powers. This will not be the case today. From Snowdon's cairn you can see, rather far below, the path (4) coming up and along the base of the steep twin peaks of Y Lliwedd. The drop to it seems perpendicular, but the hardy can go down directly without any danger. The orthodox way is to start down the Rhyd-ddu Path (1), soon turning L at a cairn to follow the Watkin Path (4) to the cross ridge dividing Cwm Tregalon from Cwm Glaslyn.

This ridge is called Bwlch y Saethau (Pass of the Arrows). The legend goes that King Arthur, having defeated his foes in the southern valley, drove them down towards Llyn Llydaw. Following them, the king was killed by a flight of arrows from the beaten foe. The misty monarch must have been as vital as a cat, judging by the number of places where he is reputed to have met a sticky end. A further tale says that a concourse of his knights lies dormant in a cave on the steep face of Lliwedd, waiting a trumpet call to renewed action.

While on Bwlch y Saethau you are not likely to meet King Arthur, but if you are very lucky you may observe a rare sight. In the late afternoon of a changeable day, when the sun is directly behind you and the vast basin below, that contains Llyn Llydaw, is filled with rolling mist curling near the tops of Y Lliwedd and Crib Goch, while rainbows come and go over the Glyders, there sometimes appears, riding on the white cloud before you, a large dark shadow in human shape. If you move from side to side the shadow does the same and if you raise your arms it follows suit. The special beauty of the spectacle is the oval halo that completely encloses the dark figure with full prismatic colours. This is the Brocken Spectre. It is used to scare the peasants of the Alps as a manifestation of the devil, but over here a more kindly legend assures the observer a front seat in heaven.

Near where you reach the bwlch it is possible to end the walk by a stiff scramble, better not attempted alone, down a rocky spine known as the Gribin (Snowdon). It projects to

Lliwedd from Bwlch y Saethau (6) - Photo L. & M. Gayt

the north-east, between the two lakes, and users should be careful to keep to its crest all the way. This is the only way off Bwlch y Saethau to the north, except by rope users. At its foot you can circle round Llydaw, using the south side, unless you are sure the causeway is not under water, which is sometimes the case in winter and wet weather. At the far end of the lake is a by-road to Pen-y-pass, that has been used by motorists (VII.ii.b).

But to complete the walk, continue along the ridge and ascend the side of Lliwedd (2,947) having all the joys of a close-up of sheer rock faces in safety L, with a gentler slope R. If it is sunny your camera should carry away some grand records of cliff and scaur. Slender and tall stand the twin peaks and you seem to be ascending the spire of some gigantic cathedral. It is perhaps the finest section of the walk.

At the time of Gladstone's visit (4), the local quarrymen raised a fine cairn on the western peak, but this has now almost disappeared, leaving barely enough shelter to protect you from any wind that blows while you admire the view. Northwards you trace with satisfaction the work already done and to the south, the winding greeness of the Gwynant Valley opens out. A short fall and rise leads to the eastern peak, whence Cwm Dyli is seen, with the well engineered road from Pen-y-Gwryd to Beddgelert above it, and this in turn is topped by the moors of Moel Siabod.

There is a well-marked path all along the crests which is helpful in thick weather. To complete the circle, follow this under the third and minor Lliwedd till a cairn is reached. Here the heights are left L for a scrambling way down grass slopes to the shores of Llyn Llydaw. Passing on to the hut that marks the end of the causeway you join the by-road winding round the north side of Llyn Teryn to Pen-y-pass. From the third Lliwedd, the whole-hogger can go yet another mile along a hummocky, grassy crest to Gallt y Wenallt (2,032) (12), which is really the very last nail in the horseshoe. For the various descents from this peak see (12).

This glorious round will take from six to eight hours and should not be hurried since every step of it is, in the word of old Baedeker, " rewarding."

CHAPTER FOUR

From Beddgelert and Rhyd-ddu

"That which gives its inexpressible charm to mountaineering is the incessant series of exquisite natural scenes, which are for the most part enjoyed by the mountaineer alone."

LESLIE STEPHEN

NOW we come to the five sections in detail, starting from the south. Beddgelert (125) is a mountain village that has entertained generations of tourists. It has an old church and a celebrated legend of a faithful hound. The Gelert or Celert after whose grave the place is named was a saint and that is about all we know of him. It is certain that the district has a very long association with the religious life of North Wales.

Beddgelert is an excellent centre for exploring the area, its only disadvantage being its lowly position, as every hill walk entails a considerable rise. All kinds of accommodation are available and special mention may be made of the Snowdonia National Forest Park Camp Site, provided by the Forestry Commission. It is an ideal place for campers and caravanners, and is situated one mile above the village on the Rhyd-ddu road.

Rhyd-ddu (626), four miles away, is a rather grim hamlet with limited quarters, but the Youth Hostel, a mile or so beyond it on the side of Llyn Cwellyn, is one of the most popular in the district.

Both places offer a variety of excursions. The approaches to Snowdon have been dealt with already. To the south-west are outlying hills with Moel Hebog as a centre; to the north-west is a long ridge walk of great merit; while eastward is a group of hills leading over to Ffestiniog, with Cnicht, the Moelwyns and some almost unknown, interesting uplands beyond. In fact the whole of Sections A and E (with the sole exception of Moel Siabod), and the greater part of Section B, can be dealt with from these two centres. Holiday makers on the southern and western fringes of Snowdonia can also reach this area with little trouble.

7. MOEL HEBOG, MOEL YR OGOF AND MOEL LEFN

Moel Hebog (hawk hill) (2,566) towers over Beddgelert and shelters it from the prevailing wind. Its ascent is a popular climb and is a fit subject for our first excursion. Go a little way up to the Rhyd-ddu road and turn L up a by-road that leads over the Afon Colwyn, twice under the disused Welsh Highland Railway, and through a small pine wood to Cwmcloch Farm. On a barn is a signpost that directs you R across a field to the rougher uplands. Some cairns will guide you up the edge of one of the shallow cwms that mark this side of the hill. It is a bit of a grind in hot weather to reach the rounded plateau that forms the summit. Near the inevitable cairn is a meeting of several stone walls that wander up and down the region, and this junction gives welcome shelter when cold breezes blow.

The view quite equals that from Snowdon, since you are on one of the seaward flanks of the whole range. To the south and west the country rolls down to the shores of Cardigan Bay, while the hills of Lleyn, the Clynnog Hills and Yr Eifl (VIII) make a fine silhouette to the west. On the other side, Beddgelert is just below and you see most of the Glaslyn Vale with Siabod (19) over Llyn Dinas. To the L of the village, the cone of Yr Aran (11) is overtopped by the twin peaks of Lliwedd (6). L again is Snowdon, with most of the Rhyd-ddu Path (1) visible. Eastwards you trace the fold that contains Aber Glaslyn Pass, and over it, Cnicht (13), a ridge from this point, and the Moelwyns (14), lead the eye to the rolling hills of Merioneth.

Various descents offer themselves. If time presses, keep due south along the edge of the cliffs L till the slope eases and then scramble east and make for the ridge leading to the cut in the pines over the Pass of Aber Glaslyn. When you see a farmhouse below, make for it and follow a track that comes out near the Goat Hotel. By making for the woods beyond the farm, you can find a path through them to the road close to the Aber Glaslyn Bridge. Holding on the ridge till it ends you have a unique view of the Pass and can get down to it L with due caution.

If the day is good and time is not a factor, keep along the edge of the cliffs to the north, descending along a wall to a wide grassy col, interspersed with boulders. Thence find your way over an open boggy area, studded with pine trees, to the corner of a mature plantation, all planted by the Forestry Commission. At the side of the latter a path runs downhill by a stream. Follow this, as near the stream as possible, till you finally reach the Snowdonia National Forest Park Camp Site, well worth inspecting for its excellent layout. The plantations will in time help to restore the wooded aspect of countryside. In olden days all the lower reaches were covered with forests of small oaks. Hence the ease with which the Welsh, including their last leader, Owain Glyndwr, evaded their English pursuers.

Talking of that famous hero, you may like to visit his Cave, which is not too easy to find. From the col under Hebog, drop a little on the Beddgelert side and work round to the first perpendicular gully. In it you will see a sort of pit dug in the cliffs. This is a disused asbestos mine. Examine it and then on the R find a rather tricky traverse that leads to the Cave in about thirty yards. It is behind a flat ledge in the cliffs, small, damp and now fern-hung. It must have been a very uncomfortable dwelling. Unless you know a bit about rock work, carefully retrace your steps to the mine before going down.

Better still do not descend just yet, but achieve two more peaks by again following the skyline above the Cave, first to the hill above it, Moel yr Ogof (hill of the cave) (2,020), and then over grass and up a small rise to the top of Moel Lefn (bald hill) (2,094), a short mile ahead. You will further enjoy the seaward view and have the renowned Pennant Valley below L. Then, skirting the westerly cliffs, go down R either to Rhyd-ddu, a long pull, or to Beddgelert, first by steep grass slopes, then out to two rocky outcrops with heathery borders and finally through the Forestry Commission land.

Visitors staying in the south can make ascents either from Pennant (VII.i.d) or Cwm Ystradllyn (VII.i.c.), both starting from the Caernarvon-Portmadoc road. The former valley is entered at Dolbenmaen Church and the hill reached by turning R at a chapel well up in the vale. At the farm Cwrt isaf, follow the stream up Cwm Llefrith to the col over Glyndwr's Cave and then R up the wall. Return by the long, long wall that runs south-west; a grand walk in the eventide.

The Cwm Ystradllyn route is not so interesting. A by-road R, two miles above Tremadoc, takes you to the lake. Ascend to the skyline, either by the disused quarry or L through a small wood marked Plasllyn on the map. Both routes are open and easily followed. An extensive water scheme has been developed in this valley.

8. THE SOUTH-WEST BUTTRESS OF SNOWDON (5 Peaks)

While on Moel Hebog a range of hills on the other side of the Pennant Valley looked most inviting, as from Moel Lefn you could almost shake hands with them. They form a series of five peaks, all over 2,000 feet, running in a more or less straight line, roughly south-west. In order, from the Snowdon end, the peaks are: Mynydd Drws-y-coed (2,286) with a spur, Y Garn, Trum y Ddysgl (2,329), Mynydd Tal-y-mignedd (2,148), Craig Cwm Silyn (2,408) and Garnedd Goch (2,301). A mile beyond the last is a rocky plateau called Mynydd Craig Goch (1,996), just outside the standard.

Y Garn, Mynydd Drws-y-Coed and Trum-y-Ddysgl (8.
Photo E. Emrys Jones

The whole lot form a somewhat curved line of about five miles and to visit all the cairns is a good day's work. Some walkers take the ridge from the far end and, facing Snowdon all day, finish at Rhyd-ddu. This is a good route, but by taking it the other way, you have an early start and the longer return at the end of the day, it all depends where your base is situated. It may be noted that visitors from the south can take the hills in two or more bites from bases in the Pennant Valley, where they will find some charming picnic sites and interesting ascents. One in particular starts behind the farm, Braich-y-dinas, and leads up a wooded gully with pools and waterfalls before it reaches the open moor under Cwm Silin.

You can reach Rhyd-ddu by bus or you can park in the new parking ground south of the village. Just opposite is a slate stile and a series of flat stones over the marsh. Follow these and soon cross a cement bridge to get on a causeway that leads to Llyn y Gader. When near the lake, turn R over a field or two and go up a grass slope that soon has cliffs R. After a good pull along the edge of these, you reach the stony top of Y Garn (not to be confused with the peak near the Devil's Kitchen). From now on, sweet upland breezes should cool your brow and a pause can be well spent in examining the panorama from this excellent vantage point (see Plate III).

To the west is a fine stretch of lowland leading to the open sea, a pleasing prospect from any high place. Caernarvon Castle stands out and a large part of Anglesey over the Menai Straits. Snowdon is very close, looking a little different as it is flanked by two of its neighbours. Yr Aran is a fine cone and, further round the three peaks ending in Moel Hebog (7) give a pretty skyline. Most striking, too, is the cleft of Drws-y-coed Pass just below, with the jagged edge of Craig y Bere, topped by Mynydd Mawr (9) on the other side.

To reach the first peak proper, you pass through a gap in the wall and work up a rocky edge with very steep grass L, dodging boulders on the way, rather like the last stages up Lliwedd (6). The crest is Mynydd Drws-y-coed. Down the other side the going is similar till more open country leads to the grassy, almost cairnless, top of the second peak, Trum y Ddysgl.

Near here there are spurs on both sides and the lay of the land makes it tricky in thick weather. Otherwise it is only necessary to make for a hefty cairn half-a-mile away, approached near the end by a narrow crest with a tiny saddle at one point. The cairn, a lofty pillar, marks the summit of Mynydd Tal-y-mignedd. At one time quarrymen made a hobby of building these miniature towers. This is one of the few points from which the three castles of Caernarvon, Criccieth and Harlech can be seen simultaneously.

As the three peaks achieved so far form a pretty trident as seen from some distant angles, there is now a considerable drop to Bwlch Drosbern, with its little-used path from Nantle to Pennant. Going down is easy, along an old wire fence, a bit steep at the base, but the ascent to Craig Cwm Silin must be taken carefully. Unless you make a wide detour R, you clamber up the edge of a fine little cliff, where the stones are apt to be loose. There is a sketchy path on the last lap to the stony summit, the highest point on the day's march. If you want to see the cliff climbs on the northern edge, go out in that direction and skirt them to the south-west to the last point.

Otherwise there is a level mile, passing two big cairns with square bases, to Garnedd Goch. Stones give way to grass and a wall guides you to the final cairn which stands amid a number of these occasional obstacles. From here you have a worthy prospect in every direction. Behind the long route you have accomplished, R lakes and a wide plain, L the depths of the Pennant Valley and before you a wide sweep of Cardigan Bay, that should be shining like "burnished gold."

It is a long way back to the starting place, but it can be regained in about two or three hours, according to pace. Work south-east over broken ground till you strike a stream and then bear east under the cliffs of Graig Las. A second stream should be followed down through a charming gully to Braich-y-dinas farm. Then turn L up the valley (VII.i.d), following farm tracks till they end and then over the lowest point in the skyline, by some disused quarries. From these a path winds round till you see Llyn Gader and the village well below. Here you can find a way R to Beddgelert or make direct to Rhyd-ddu. In either case there are Forestry Commission plantations to be negotiated.

Alternatively, but longer, keep north of the wall that comes up to the cairn and drop down to an old quarrymen's path and soon bear R northward to have a hard slog over a wide moor on about the 1,000 foot contour, leaving the twin lakes of Cwm Silin R and later, Llyn Nantlle-uchaf well down on the L. You skirt the base of all the peaks visited and strike the main road well up the Drws-y-coed Pass. From the top of the Pass to Rhyd-ddu is about a mile (9).

Thirdly, much footwork can be saved and a new cwm visited by making direct for Llyn Cwm-Dulyn to the west, over easy grassy slopes. Keep on the north side of the lake and, at the far end, with its stone dam, you will find a track leading to the biblically named villages of Nebo and Nazareth, marked from above by a row of new white houses. From the hamlets it is a short mile to the main Caernarvon-Portmadoc road, with a bus service to either town.

Finally you can bag yet another peak by dropping down the wall to the south until a cross wall is met then working round the head of Cwm Dulyn with its lake and crags, to reach the flattish top of Mynyd Craig Goch (1,996), where your head at least will surmount 2,000 feet. This miniature Glyder is the very last point of Snowdonia to the south-west and the view is a reward for the extra labour.

Leave the hill to the north-west for the village of Nazareth, near a line of power poles, by-passed by a farm track on either side. The way off due south is very bad going and should be avoided. It is very boggy on the east side if you are making for Portmadoc, but a way can be found, the cone shaped Craig y Garn (1,190) acting as a pointer to the entrance of the Pennant Valley.

It has not been easy to describe the way to explore this fine stretch of country. In any case the weary can drop off at many points, but it is no trip for a misty day. You have been warned!

9. MYNYDD MAWR

Mynydd Mawr (2,291) is the last peak to be visited in Section A. It is somewhat isolated between the Caernarvon-Beddgelert road and Drws-y-coed Pass and it looks well as you come from Beddgelert to Rhyd-ddu. To explore it is a pleasant half-day trip without much excitement. The views are similar to those from the south-west buttress (8), but there are a lot of quarry workings close at hand and the bulk of Snowdon cuts off a good deal of the panorama. Coming up from Beddgelert, turn L in Rhyd-ddu village up a steepish hill that leads to Nantlle Vale. A mile or so on, park at the top of the Pass, as near a lake R as you can.

This lake is Llyn-y-Dywarchen, known as the lake of the floating island. It has an odd twisted shape and the lump of turbary on one of its sides does not float nowadays, in spite of the legend confirmed by Pennant some two hundred years ago. At its west end, where the lake is close to the road, near a small building, cross the embankment and then swing L through a miniature rocky pass, with a path to guide you. Near another corner of the lake you can bear L up an easy grass slope rising before you. There is a more direct scramble further L, but it is better to work up the easier gradient. As you rise the crest narrows somewhat and a wide cwm opens out R, while on the L are the sharp cliffs of Craig y Bere. They are jagged enough to remind you of the Devil's Kitchen, but the rock is too loose for climbing.

From the top you can peer down into the narrow valley of Drws-y-coed (gate of the wood). Today there are no woods, only a bare valley, a disused copper mine and a few cottages. In the small hamlet, you can pick out the huge boulder on the far side of the road that practically demolished a chapel when it fell from Y Garn (8) some years ago. A new chapel was built in a safer place on the other side of tho road, mainly by contributions from the curious who always flock to the scene of a disaster. There is another tale about the valley, from the far-off days when it was full of oak trees. It is said that a forest fire broke out at either end and that many animals perished in the flames, their cries filling the air.

You can follow a long sheep track round the edge of the cwm till a double cairn that marks the real summit shows up R. The outline of the hill, as seen from Caernarvon, gives it the name of Elephant Mountain and the summit is the centre of its back, which is certainly broad enough. Continue north over heather and dwarf bilberries to another cairn that marks the top of the head, with a steep drop down to Llyn Cwellyn. There is little trace of Castell Cidwm (wolf's castle) although its site is an obvious strong-point. Legend says that a giant, Cidwm, shot an arrow from it to slay a prince invading his lands from South Wales.

There is the usual choice of descents. From the main summit there is an easy grass slope to the nearest and highest slate quarry passing near the tarn Llyn y Ffynhonau. If time allows turn L near the tarn to explore the rugged slate quarries of the Nantlle Vale. Here slate was heaved up out of huge pits and the waste thrown on one side, till in the course of years it has submerged acres of land and not a few cottages. A fortune awaits the man who can find a profitable use for this awkward debris. You can avoid this grim region by bearing R round the edge of the northern cwm and taking a rough course over stony ground that leads to the upper end of Bettws-Garmon, a charming wooded village, with some fine falls in private grounds, where visitors are welcome and also a Holiday Home.

You can reach your base on the Pass either by retracing your steps, or, better, scramble east through heather to the stream below, then head straight for the top of Yr Aran (11) and later bear R through some new Forestry Commission plantations. Over a very modest skyline you soon reach some point on Llyn y Dywarchen and the base is just round the corner. Incidentally there is a way to the Snowdon Ranger Youth Hostel down the stream passed in this descent, but Llyn Cwellyn has to be circled.

10. MOEL CYNGHORION, FOEL GRON AND MOEL EILIO

Before leaving the Rhyd-ddu region a little poaching in the Llanberis area is justified, since these three hills can be tackled from this side with advantage. Their approach is rather easier and a rewarding climax is attained at an early stage. They form the north-west spur of Snowdon and, while less difficult than the south-west, they furnish a more interesting profile of the central Massif.

The start is from the Youth Hostel on Llyn Cwellyn and follows (3) as far as the line of power poles. Here the slope flattens out and a narrow path goes over to Llanberis at the side of the poles (VII.ii.h). Take this till you reach an iron gate and then leave it R up grass slopes to pass over a wide plateau. At its far end you are on Moel Cynghorion (hill of the councillors) (2,207). There is certainly room for all the wise men in the world on its broad crest.

Before you, with a sharp drop to the east, is a very fine view. Llanberis with its lakes and huge quarries is seen down a wide valley, while up the opposite ridge runs the toy train that bears the lazy to Snowdon Summit. The rugged skyline above the ridge hides the Pass of Llanberis. Fine cwms flank either side, the one R, with a string of small tarns at its base, has some of the hardest rock climbs in Britain (3). The edge of the Glyders (16), with the tip of Tryfan (20) L, rise sharply over the hidden Pass, while Snowdon itself crowns the prospect.

For the next point retrace your footsteps for a short mile to the Llanberis traverse and turn R along an obvious up and down skyline. The first "up", marked Foel Goch on the map, barely reaches 2,000 feet, although most of the ridge hovers about that contour. The next crest, Foel Gron (2,100) has sharp crags on the Llanberis side and from it a grassy rise along the edge of the ridge. This shapely and outstanding hill is a fitting end to the buttress. It commands yet another of those satisfying views from an outlying point.

Llanberis shelters just below and can be reached in half-an-hour down a gentle slope of springy turf ending in a drop to the crofts near the railway, the Victoria Hotel being a guide to the direct descent. It is also easy to drop down, a little more steeply, to the shores of Llyn Dwythwch R (VII.ii.h), but the ground round the lake is marshy and it lies shut in by the sides of a rather dull cwm. By either route you pass near one of the finest falls in Wales, formed by the busy waters of the Afon Arddu as it runs down to the Llanberis lakes.

If you happen to be on your way to Caernarvon, take a line direct to its Castle and drop down till you see slate workings a little L. Passing through these you will find a track leading to a good by-road and, a mile on, to Waenfawr Post Office, where buses pass. In reverse this is a good way up to the ridge.

The cairn on Moel Eilio is made of rocks that somehow seem to collect on many tops. Judging by the number that often are placed in a circle, it seems very possible that they were used by ancient Welsh "Commandos." From this particular point they would cover quite a stretch of the lowlands running over to Anglesey.

The return to Rhyd-ddu is a simple matter. Just walk off the hill in a southerly direction selecting a grass slope, or go down one of the groves cut in the hillside by little streams and so regain the main road at any desired point, to walk up the hill to the village. This trip is well suited for a hot day. The going is easy and all the way the views are good enough to give every excuse for many halts.

11. YR ARAN

Yr Aran (the height) (2,451), the hill that commands Nant Gwynant, is visible from a wide stretch of country and stands right between Beddgelert and Snowdon. In coming up to the village from Portmadoc, it is often taken for its neighbour when cloud wreathes the giant. It can be combined with the ascent of Snowdon by routes 1 or 4, but it is well worth a half-day trip on its own.

Take the Capel Curig road from Beddgelert. In a mile you pass the grassy and wooded mound of Dinas Emrys L, full of legends of King Arthur and his familiar spirit, Merlin. It is an obvious strongpoint and if you scramble to its top you will find traces of old buildings, that have been excavated lately.

Just beyond it, in the curve of the road, is a farm track leading through a gate to Hafod-y-Porth farm. Before the house is reached, turn R through some sheep pens and over a grass avenue between bracken. Soon there is an ancient trackway by a stream. Carry on by two lonely stone posts and, higher, the roofless ruins of a steading are passed and then an old copper mine, with retaining wall, horizontal shaft and piles of brown waste. This is half-a-mile south of the "Mine disused" on the map. Here there are two streams and the L one should be followed, till you feel inclined to leave its rather swampy banks to make for the skyline above. As is usual this is wide and irregular when attained, but when rusty iron posts are sighted, make for them as they are the remains of a fence that once ran right over the summit to prevent sheep falling over the sharp cliffs to the north. The small cairn on the sharp peak that forms the top gives a noble all-round view.

Here are the peaks, working R from Snowdon: Crib Goch, Glyders, Lliwedd, Wenallt, Siabod, Moel Meirch, Penamnen, Arenigs, Moel yr Hydd, Cnicht, Moelwyns, Cader Idris, Rhinogs, Moel ddu, Hebog, Ogof, Lefn, Southwest Buttress hills, Mynydd Mawr and Eilio with its neighbours, to say nothing of the many lakes and the ocean beyond Portmadoc.

Perhaps the best descent is by the south-west, keeping as high as possible on good grass, over a minor height, Craig Wen (1,984) with Moel Hebog (7) and the sunset before you. By aiming at the top of Hebog, you will come out on the Rhyd-ddu road, just opposite the Snowdon National Forest Park Camp Site, one mile above Beddgelert. By bearing L on the lower stages you can find a stiffer, but more direct way to the village. Indeed the whole south side of Yr Aran is wild and rough. It is, however, quite easy to go east, near a wall running along the moderate cliffs in that direction and drop down to the Watkin path (4), making towards the ruined house near the Gladstone Rock. Then descend by an old incline to the Chalet and the main road. Any more direct route will land you in confusing pathless woods west of the Chalet.

12. GALLT Y WENALLT

Gallt y Wenallt (2,032) is not in the official list, doubtless because it is considered part of Lliwedd. However it is now included since it has a crest and is a mile from its higher neighbour. In any case its ascent makes a delightful half-day trip from Beddgelert.

Commence at the Watkin Path (4) and, when near the Chalet, turn down R to Hafodllan farm, where there are good camping sites. Just beyond the farmyard, turn L over a cement bridge. Passing between two wooden chalets, the path goes R through the woodlands beside a gurgling stream, with some considerable falls. At the end of the woods, bear R away from the stream and rise into open country. Get out on the ridge and Llyn Gwynant will appear well below. You are now on the skyline that looks so well from the main road but, like many others, this is no knife edge, but a wide upland with numerous hummocks, that can be surmounted or circumvented to reach the topmost rocky point.

Again there is a grand prospect, since you are at the very tip of the Horseshoe (6) and get a fine view of its sweep. Snowdon dominates the scene with Crib Goch to the R. Under its shadow you can trace the Zigzags and the Pig Track (5). The Glyders (16) and Moel Siabod (19) fill the horizon to the north and east and then a series of crests lead the eye round to the ridge of Cnicht (13).

The shortest way back is to make for a stream to the south-west and follow it by some old mine workings, unseen from any high road. Where moor, woods, water and wall all meet at a dingle, the outward path is regained. If traversing to Pen-y-Gwryd you can take a long slant down to the black pipe lines from Llyn Llydaw and on to the Cwm Dyli Power

Station (VII.ii.a). Due east from the top are some of the steepest grassy slopes in the district and you must be sure-footed to go down them. With time in hand, do not resist the temptation to renew acquaintance with Lliwedd (6), reached by a fine walk along the edge of steep cliffs. From either peak it is possible to drop down near the Gladstone Rock over some very broken ground, but it will probably save time to go down the Horseshoe track to Bwlch y Saethau and follow the regular Watkin Path to the Beddgelert road.

Section E is the most remote from the busy north coast resorts, but is easily accessible from the south. It is dealt with here because Beddgelert is as good a centre as any for exploring all its peaks, except Moel Siabod, an isolated point in the north of the section.

13. CNICHT

Portmadoc, with a circle of mountains to the north, is faintly reminiscent of Innsbruck, but the town has a smiling sea to the south, which the continental city cannot rival. In any case from the main streets of the Welsh town you can see the perfect cone of Cnicht (knight) (2,265). Borrow calls it " the conical peak impaling heaven " and more flattering observers term it " the Matterhorn of Wales." At all events it **looks** a mountain and is well worth climbing. Most ascents are made up a by-road from Garreg a village on the east side of the Glaslyn Vale, to Croesor and up the side that faces Portmadoc. This is a good route and not so difficult as it looks.

But from Beddgelert there is a more varied ascent. Just outside the village leave the Capel Curig road R over a newish bridge. Here are the last ruins of the old mill that many artists, including the famous David Cox, used to paint in the old days. Turn L up the valley keeping to the track near the river. When Llyn Dinas is reached go R along its edge after crossing a small stream. The paths on the map are vague and you must work R through a copse beneath a distinctive hilltop R, crowned with a bunch of firs. The way passes near Hafod Owen farm, a lonely cottage and another copse, to reach a by-road at a chapel. It is possible to reach this point by car or cycle, by leaving the Capel Curig road R over a cement bridge at the foot of the hill beyond Dinas and driving up a pretty but narrow road with gates. The parking space at the chapel is very limited.

Pausing to admire the Snowdon group from an unusual angle go 300 yards L and turn R down a track to a large farmstead R to pick up a path that ascends near a lively brook, cascading down. Then the ground levels out a bit and is rather boggy, till you reach Llyn Llagi (1,238), the roundest little tarn in all the world. The waters of Llyn Adar, 600 feet higher, fall in a straight line into it. Ardent scramblers can find a way up beside the falls to the skyline, but the easier way to the ridge is R from the lower lake up a less steep watercourse. You will be glad when the top is reached and then, leaving the oval Llyn Biswail L, skirt the edge of the screes and make for the R of the three rounded crests ahead. In a few minutes the summit of Cnicht is yours.

Once again the view from an outlying peak is superb. To the south green pastures with the Glaslyn wandering through them, lead the eye to the mile-long Portmadoc Embankment and the open sea beyond. Over to the south-west are seen the far-away hills of Lleyn, while west and north stands the mighty range of Snowdon. To the east, separated only by a grim narrow valley, are the fine outlines of the Moelwyns, while the Merioneth coast, with the towers of Harlech Castle, backed by the Rhinogs, with the top stages of Cader Idris above them, complete a circle of beauty.

Those based on the chapel can retrace their steps or amuse themselves exploring a low rocky plateau containing three tarns to the west, finding their way down where the slope eases, meeting rough going most of the way. Others finding that the view from Portmadoc was deceptive, and that the peak is only the end of a long ridge, can walk along this till a way down R is found, for preference at the end of the scree, into Cwm Croesor, the grim hollow, made grimmer by quarry workings. A small lake, with a dam, a stream, a water pipe and traces of quarry paths show the descent till the bottom is reached and then an old tramway leads to Croesor village.

Alternatively, Croesor can be reached by steering direct for Portmadoc. The first drop is steep, but later, you can work round a series of hummocks and slip down L by a small farm to the village. Thence a charming track, said to be of Roman origin, leads in a north-westerly direction to Aberglaslyn Bridge and so to Beddgelert (VII.i.h).

Croesor, in a cul-de-sac, can be reached by car, through a public road which is very narrow. It commences **under the** pretty lodge of Plas-brondanw, close to the village of Garreg on the eastern side of the Glaslyn Vale. Its nearest bus stop is at Tanlan, in a sharp angle of the road from Garreg to Aberglaslyn.

14. MOELWYN FAWR, MOELWYN BACH AND MOEL YR HYDD

Across the valley from Cnicht (13) there was a close up view of Moelwyn, Mawr (2,527) and Bach (2,334), with Craig Ysgafn between them. They are the most southerly of all Snowdonia and, since there is a steep drop from them to the Vale of Ffestiniog, they make a stout rampart. Indeed, when covered with snow they appear much higher than the figures on the map.

To traverse them makes a fine skyline walk, which should be started from Croesor (13). From the village there is a track, hair-raising for motorists or even cyclists, leading to a disused quarry some 1,500 feet up which saves time if Moelwyn Mawr only is your object. However, for the round trip, leave the transport at the base and trudge up the track for a mile or so. Where a small stream runs under the road, turn R up a steep grassy slope, between rocks that form a minor cwm, till a ridge is reached. Proceed along the ridge with a steady rise to the small cairn on the summit of the Mawr.

From the top the view is similar, but more extensive, than that from Cnicht (13), as it also includes the green Vale of Ffestiniog, the vast slate workings round Blaenau Ffestiniog, more of the wild lands of Merioneth, part of Llyn Trawsfynydd (the largest artificial lake in Wales) and the lonely dignity of Moel Siabod. These lists are getting a bit monotonous, but it is good to see old friends from new angles and pick out fresh features from different standpoints.

As you stretch your legs on the wide expanse of good turf, you may be tempted to bag yet another peak to the north-east. It is Moel yr Hydd (stag's head) (2,124). The way is clear along the edge of a moor, with a drop R that holds Llyn Stwlan. In a mile or so you reach the cairn after a small rise, and you note that the stag has a bald head. From it you see Llyn Cwmorthin (15), shut in by a circle of hills.

If you want to come off the hill, you can drop down to the lake, either north by a small brook or, with more scrambling, to the east. In both cases you finish down a slate road with pretty waterfalls that leads to Tan-y-grisiau, a suburb of Blaenau Ffestiniog, with a bus service to that centre. The area is now much changed since the construction of the pumped storage scheme, with the huge dam at Llyn Stwlan, the power house and the large artificial lake.

But it is time to get on with the main task. In returning to Moelwyn Mawr, you might like to examine the huge pits of abandoned slate quarries R. Use care because the pits and the shaft nearby are unfenced. All round this region there is evidence of much capital sunk in looking for slate and other minerals in the palmy days of the native quarry industries.

Passing on from the summit of the Mawr to the Bach, you go down a steep grass slope to the crags of Craig Ysgafn. There is a reasonably easy way over these, only the descent to the col below the Bach needing care, or there is an obvious path R under them that leads to the same col. Thence a detour is necessary to reach the top, either L slanting over scree followed by a sharp rise up grass, or wider to the R up grass gullies. On the summit you are, as it were, on the top of the world, with the finest view of the Vale of Ffestiniog. It is " furthest south " and you should go over to the last rocky spur to complete the good work before considering the descent.

There is a good easy grass slope, with small cliffs L, running west that lands you on the Roman road (VII.i.h), about a mile from Croesor R. The lower stages are boggy and the path shown on the map is not easy to find. For the more energetic there are sporting descents on the rougher sides of the hill, either by a scramble down to Llyn Stwlan and then by quarry paths to Tan-y-grisiau or, better from the spur, southwards as directly as possible, to two small tarns, Llyn y Garnedduchaf, clearly visible from the top. The ground is rough and boggy in places and the start is steep. After skirting the lakes, you should pick up a farm path by a stream that leads to the farm, Creuau, just above Tan-y-bwlch station of the Ffestiniog Railway. Enthusiasts have recently opened the narrow-guage railway up to this point and you can enjoy a run down to Portmadoc in its miniature coaches during the summer months. From the platform you can go through an iron gate R, and follow a wall to reach the Roman road in a short distance. It is a pleasant saunter of about three miles back to Croesor.

If not due back at this base, a path L, also from the station, runs sharply down to charming Llyn Mair. From its wooded shores the main road goes down a steep hill to the Oakley Arms Hotel, near Maentwrog, with a frequent bus service either to Portmadoc or Ffestiniog.

15. ALLT FAWR AND MOEL DRUMAN

Section E has two very out-of-the-way peaks. They are

over the valley from Moel yr Hydd (14). A visit to them makes an interesting day, since it brings you to some secluded lakes and opens out country that is seldom explored. Blaenau Ffestiniog makes the best starting place and cars can be parked near the Railway Station. If taken further up they are awkward to regain. Unlike Llanberis, where the sides of the hills are quarried in the open, or Nantlle Vale where the slate is hauled out of deep pits, the Ffestiniog quarries consist of sixty miles of workings, mainly underground. Thus only the waste appears on the surface.

Follow the Betws-y-coed road, through towering masses of this waste, till the road rises and surmounts it, reaches open country and goes over the Crimea Hill. In just over a mile and shortly before the top, there is a small lake below L, Llyn Fridd-y-bwlch, and the road is left to cross the embankment at its south end. Then bear R round a grass rise till you see an obvious hollow L. Make your way up this by a faint path to a smaller tarn, Llyn Iwerddon, also with a small embankment.

On the way you crossed over the railway tunnel, whose entrance dated 1879, was noted from the main road as you came up. It is two miles long and connects Ffestiniog with the Lledr Valley. The second lake is at the head of the cwm and there is a short rise to the ridge above it. This marks the county boundary between Caernarvon and Merioneth and from the whole of its length you have a very pleasing prospect.

The point attained is near the southern edge of the widest cwm of all. The other end, nearly five miles away, is bounded by Moel Siabod (19). Between stretches the lonely upper part of the Lledr Valley. All the six streams that unite to form the delightful river after which the vale is named rise in this wide space. It is not a long pull up the ridge to the top of Allt Fawr (2,287), whence there is a feast of good things, including a grand view of the Moelwyns from the north.

West of the hill, you pass down to a largish lake, Llyn Conglog (angular lake) (2,002), the highest one of its size. It is an impressive sheet, especially as the writer saw it one sunny day in January, covered with a light pall of snow over bearable ice. The only marks on the whole surface were the footprints of a mountain hare startled a few minutes earlier. Skirt close to the lake to reach Moel Druman (ridge mountain) (2,152) only a little higher than the lake. The few rocks on the flat top make a good luncheon place. You can amuse yourself trying to count the tarns and lakes in sight and you will be surprised to see so much of the Glaslyn Vale between the higher peaks.

Once again there is a varied choice of descents. If bound to return to Blaenau Ffestiniog, you must follow on round Llyn Conglog, dodging down small cliffs to some quarry workings with small lakes all around them. Thence there is a rough road southwards to Llyn Cwmorthin (14) almost 1,000 feet lower than Conglog, only half-a-mile above. The former lake is well shut in, with only an odd farm or two and a closed chapel on its shores. The track runs along it and down by more quarry works to Tan-y-grisiau (14), a mile from Blaenau Ffestiniog, with a possible bus. In this region a power station has been built, considerably altering the lay of the land near Tan-y-grisiau.

Freelances can find an obvious way by Llyn Croesor to a quarry, where explosives have been stored, and reach Croesor village by the track mentioned in (14). In following this route you will be in the track of that famous traveller, Pennant. Two hundred years ago he crossed on horseback from Cwmorthin to Croesor and wrote: " We met with such narrowness of path, such short turnings and horrible precipices, that our poor beasts trembled at every limb and, in fact, had a wonderful escape in getting safely to the bottom." Things are not quite so bad today, at least for the pedestrian, since generations of quarrymen have worn footpaths through most of the cols.

Strong walkers without a base are heartily recommended to continue right round the top of the ridge, aiming at the summit of Snowdon for nearly two miles. The going is fairly level at about the two thousand contour. As you pass behind Cnicht its outline changes—first a ridge, then a cone, later a trident and finally a double peak. In broken country a group of tiny lakes is passed and later Llyn Edno, that loneliest haunt of anglers. It is so hidden in hummocks L that it is not easily found, but it is worth finding since there is a jolly way to lower levels by the stream that runs out of the south side of Edno westwards to the road that comes up from the highway between Llyn Dinas and Llyn Gwynant (13).

There is some sort of a fisherman's path to help through the rocks and, when the country opens out, you should make for the edge of woodlands R, to reach the road near a farm-house. To the north of Edno is the stony plateau of Moel Meirch (1,998), the highest of the " also rans." If you visit its summit, you will get quite a new outline of the Snowdon group. From it there is a way through very broken country down to Llyn Gwynant, where the compass is useful. These last two descents land you at remote places.

Sticking to the main ridge, which is called Ysgafell Wen

(the white rim) there is another mile to the north-east along to Yr Arddu (1,933), with a wide hollow before you leading to Moel Siabod (19). In a bog half-a-mile due west of Yr Arddu an Irish 'plane crashed with tragic loss of life in 1952.

You can now drop down R on grass to the scattered hamlet of Roman Bridge, with its Youth Hostel and railway station. The latter is useful, since there may be a train to Blaenau Ffestiniog, so that you can regain your base after a wonderful circular walk, mainly at a high level.

CHAPTER FIVE

From Pen-y-Gwryd, Pen-y-Pass and Llanberis

"But happily to most of us the great brown slabs bending over into immeasurable space, the lines and curves of the wind-moulded cornice, the delicate undulations of the fissured snow, are old and trusted friends, ever luring us to health and fun and laughter and enabling us to bid a sturdy defiance to all the ills that time and life oppose."

A. F. MUMMERY

ALL the peaks within reach of Beddgelert have now been visited and an ascent must be made to wilder regions around the middle watershed. It is necessary to pass up the famous Vale of Nant Gwynant (VII.ii.a), eight miles of varied beauty. The first half is fairly level, but after the second lake, a long rise up a well engineered road leads on to Pen-y Gwryd (900) and in a further mile to Pen-y-pass (1,169). A mile before Pen-y-Gwryd there is a grand view of most of the Horseshoe (6) from the outside L. The two places were both isolated hotels having long associations with walkers and climbers. In fact they were the twin nurseries of cliff climbing in Wales, since Ogwen came into the picture rather later. Pen-y-Gwryd is still a thriving hotel and is also a Mountain Rescue Post.

Pen-y-pass is now a modern Youth Hostel and cafe. However, Llanberis (340), over five miles down the Pass from Pen-y-pass, is the centre for most visitors. Here an extensive slate quarry industry does not repel tourists. On the contrary, its fine situation, with a wealth of mountains on three sides, its renowned Pass, its twin lakes and its Snowdon

Mountain Railway, attracts more people every year. Quarters of every kind, from Youth Hostels to modern hotels, are available and the frequent bus service from Caernarvon, as well as numerous motor coach tours, make it a rendezvous for day trippers.

From the three places a great variety of excursions can be made. They include Snowdon and its near neighbours (1-6), mostly with well marked paths; the Glyders (16), all heather rocks and plateaux; Y Garn and Foel Goch (17), outlying peaks on the northern spur; the Elidirs (18), mixed grass and stones as well as a wealth of shorter walks. After the trips around the southern edge, you are back again amongst the giants.

While the hills to the south of Llanberis have already been dealt with (10), there are variations of merit from this side, especially from the track of the Mountain Railway, and the vale below it. They give traverses to Llyn Cwellyn at different levels (VII.ii.h). Those equal to rough scrambling should not omit a visit to Cwm Glas (VII.ii.e) and cross over to Llyn Llydaw under Crib Goch (6). These and other walks are given in (VII.ii).

16. THE GLYDERS, NAMELESS PEAK AND GALLT YR OGOF

Glyder Fawr (3,279) and Glyder Fach (3,262) (great and little pile), are well named. Such a waste of rocks and boulders, scattered over a platform more than a mile long, is seldom found. It, and the Carneddau ridge (23), are the two highest connected land areas south of the Border. When tackling the heaped stones on these heights one feels like a mouse exploring a coal cellar, but without the wee beastie's agility. Pennant had this to say of them: " Numerous groups of stones are placed almost erect, sharp pointed and in shafts: all are weather beaten, time-eaten, and honeycombed, and of a venerable grey colour."

The plateau is, *pace* Snowdon, the real centre of the whole mountain mass. It frowns down on Llanberis Pass, and there are open views to the south and east with Siabod's huge flanks and on the northern bastions are the peaks of Tryfan (20), Y Garn and Foel Goch (17). To explore the whole area would need a week of fine days, but it should be avoided in misty weather, because there are few marked paths and the drop on the northern side is mostly very sheer. While Snowdon swarms with people at all holiday times and stray walkers are found there on most fine days, these hills are comparatively deserted except for those who go to high lonely places for their special charm.

The slightly marked summits can be reached by many routes. The easiest ascent is described, with a note of some variation. Park the car or cycle at Pen-y-Gwryd Hotel and, just beyond, leave the Capel Curig road L just beyond a bridge, to make for a wall L that runs up the rather dull looking hillside over damp ground. Keep near this for a while and, after a gap in a cross wall, marked with white stones, you will find the regular path with cairns that goes up through rocks and heather. An hour's grind will bring you to a boggy plain, with a few flat stones laid on the wettest parts. At its far end is a large cairn and a pause is imposed to note a grand all-round view of the hills that have, heretofore, been mainly hidden.

Filling the foreground is that perfect mountain, Tryfan. Its equal rocky sides rise to a tri-part peak. On the highest of these the twin rocks, Adam and Eve, stand out clearly. You will hear more of them later on. If binoculars are carried, probably you will be able to pick out parties of climbers, since the steep faces opposite are criss-crossed with rock routes, all taped and noted in little books.

On the R of Tryfan rise the rounded summits of the mighty Carneddau. Beyond are the faint outlines of the Denbigh Moors, while to the south Moel Siabod (19) fills a great part of the horizon. But Tryfan dominates the prospect and the first impulse is to follow the clear path that goes down from the cairn, work round the rough cwm and reach its summit from the higher end of the Heather Terrace (20). This route in its early stages is the Miners' Track (VII.iii.e) and is much used, especially in a traverse from the Ogwen area to Nant Gwynant. But the Glyders are today's objective. Even so there is a grassy detour that shall be described before they are tackled in earnest, since this is a good starting point for two other peaks on the list.

To the R of the ridge where you sit, is a small tarn, Caseg-fraith (piebald maro). Skirt this and go due east till you reach the Nameless Peak (2,636) and then bear a little to the north for Gallt yr Ogof (the slope of the cave) (2,499). Both of these hills furnish fine open views down to Capel Curig and beyond and, on the other side, you see through a gap right across to the sea at the mouth of the Glaslyn. From the latter cairn, if you wish to get down to Capel Curig, you must swing R or L to avoid some steep cliffs. At the base of these you can reach Ogwen on the near side of Afon Llugwy (VII.iii.d). The cave that names the hill is in the cliffs, but is not very imposing. Again by going south, over a lower ridge, you can come out on the main road near the twin lakes, Llynnau Mymbyr.

astell-y-Gwynt and Glyder Fawr - Photo L. & M. Gayton

All the land to the south of this ridge, in fact the whole of that side of the Glyders, is part of the farm of Dyffryn Mymbyr, made famous in that wartime best seller, **I Bought a Mountain**. The book gives an excellent all-round picture of life in the Welsh hills and is well worth reading.

This pleasant spur of the Glyders is not often visited, as the higher peaks are more attractive, but it furnishes a good alternative should the latter become cloud-capped.

It is high time that the main task is pursued. Turn L from the cairn up a stony way, with some sort of path, along or near the cliff edge R, till the top of Glyder Fach is reached. Mild gymnastics are required to explore the heaped pile of gigantic boulders that compose the summit. You will notice one flat projecting table stone, called "the Cantilever," that looks as if a strong wind would dislodge it. Yet Tennant recorded it **in situ** nearly two hundred years ago and probably it has not moved for thousands.

It is a stony path that leads over to the three separate cairns that mark the top of Glyder Fawr and you lose little height as you go. On the way you pass Castell y Gwynt R another mass of big rocks, near the upper end of Y Gribin (Glyders).

Here is a true story of this very spot. Some years ago, two climbers were taking lunch in the shelter of a rock, having been caught in thick mist after a sunny morning. Peering through the gloom, one of them remarked: "Well, that's the first sheep I've seen with a square head." "That's not a sheep," said the other, so they went over to investigate. Seated on another rock they found a man eating biscuits out of a brief case. He was dressed in a black tail coat and striped trousers and wore light shoes and a top hat. Saluting him, the climbers asked if they could be of any service. "Not at all," said the stranger. "You see it's like this—I'm a barrister, due in Liverpool Court, and I crossed from Dublin in the night boat. The light over Snowdon caught my eye from the train, so I sent a wire from Bangor to say I'd been delayed. And then I came up here to get that grand view to the south and have been punished for my sin by this counfounded mist." These hills certainly are magnetic!

Authorities agree that the view from the Glyders is one of the finest in Snowdonia, because the four long valleys stretching out below give a sense of space from a mighty platform. The Conway Valley runs down to the sea near Great Orme; Nant Ffrancon shows Penrhyn Castle and the Menai Straits; Llanberis

Pass opens out Caernarvon and most of Anglesey and, finally, Nant Gwynant leads to Traeth and the sea below Harlech. Moreover the grim cliffs to the north make an imposing foreground on that side.

Before saying farewell to these engaging heights some ascents from the north may be given. Any of these can be used for the descent. The best way up from Llanberis leaves the main Pass just beyond Nant Peris (VII.ii.f). At the top of the Devil's Kitchen, go over to Llyn y Cwn and, leaving it R, you pick up a cairned path through the loose scree that will land you on top of the Fawr.

Ogwen walkers will find the easiest way to the Fach by the Miners' Track (20 and VII.iii.e) up to the cairn where Tryfan came into view on the way up from Pen-y-Gwryd, and then follow the route already given. From the cwm below Tryfan you can use the Bristly Ridge. This popular scramble is well marked by boot scratches, but it should only be attempted with a companion who knows it. It makes a much better ascent than descent. The scree to its east can be run down, but it is very toilsome to ascend. The Ridge or the scree comes out very near the summit of Fach.

Those not seeking thrills should try Y Gribin (Glyders) which can be started by bearing R after half-a-mile of the Miners' Track from Ogwen and getting to the top of a grass spur that holds Llyn Bochlwyd. There are many paths up this ridge, that stands between the lake and the Nameless Cwm. Keep on its crest and the going is easy except for one or two sharp rises near the top, where care is needed. The plateau is reached among the rocks near Castell y Gwynt. On the other side of the Nameless Cwm is the Senior Ridge, which can be started from the south-east side of Llyn Idwal. It presents no difficulty and brings you to that wide open space that surrounds the small cairns of the Fawr. From above it will be seen that the forbidding north side can be tackled without much trouble.

On the other sides there is a variety of descents. The one along the ridge from the Fach to Capel Curig has been dealt with already. If you want to get back to Pen-y-Gwryd from the Fawr, turn south from the cairns and work down the stream that runs into Llyn Cwm-y-ffynnon. This shallow hollow is called the Heather Gully and entails rough, but not steep, going. From the lake, follow the skyline west from the Fawr, till the dangerous drop of Esgair Felen halts you. Then, with a fine bird's eye view of the Pass, work along the grass well above the lake to drop directly down to Pen-y-pass.

It will be seen that this great plateau affords much variety.

Whatever route is followed, few trips give greater satisfaction than a day on the Glyders, provided only that the weather is reasonable.

17. FOEL GOCH AND Y GARN

Moel Siabod is the only height left within reach of the two hotels, but as this is more amusing from Capel Curig, descend to Llanberis to clear up the middle area. The hills to the south-west of the town have been described (10), except for variations left to your own inclination. On the north-east there are six summits which can be taken in two excellent all-day outings. Of course they can all be tackled together by the tigers or split up into shorter sections by the more modest. The first two to be visited, Foel Goch (2,727) and Y Garn (3,104) are linked up with the Glyders (16) to some extent. They are often done from Ogwen, but climbed from the south side they give a more effective climax.

From Llanberis, make your way by the side of Llyn Peris up the Pass for two miles. Nearly oposite the tiny church at Nant Peris, leave the road L and thread your way by track through the small crofts on the hillside till more open country is reached. Follow up Afon Gafr, the R of the two brooks that come down the cwm, leaving the masses of slate waste on the other side of the smooth hollow. The going is good but the way seems long up to the two-mile pull to the cairn on Foel Goch (red hill). Here you stand at the centre of five cwms, two with grassy sides and three with relatively sheer drops. The ridge walk westwards to Elidir Fawr looks tempting, but today's route is the other way, where the view across Nant Ffrancon is wild and rugged, in complete contrast to the grassy side just accomplished.

The rocky cwms, each divided from the next by buttresses of cliff, run out to narrow meadows in the vale far below, with the stream and main road beyond them. Up this road comes civilisation in car and coach, scanning the hills from cushioned seats, only leaving them for a hasty glance at the Ogwen Falls at the lower end of the lake. We can also see remote Llyn Idwal and most of the northern cliffs of the Glyders, with Tryfan beyond. The Carneddau too, rise sharply from the other side of the vale and you realise their vast extent. On either side of Elidir Fawr the slate heaps of Llanberis and Bethesda fill the northern horizon.

Now turn south for a walk along a bracing mile-long sky-line that rises to Y Garn. A rest is needed by the large cairn on this second peak, especially to admire the grim aspect of the Snowdon Group across the Pass and to study the various routes up the cliffs of the Glyders. Y Garn has been well termed "a fine view point and a shapely peak." A rounded cone from this side, it is sharply cut off on the other, and shows a sheer face to Ogwen. The war left its traces even in these remote places. Not far from the top, too high for salvage, lie rusty fragments of a war plane—not the only one in these regions.

From the summit you can make a bee line for Nant Peris, without any steep gradients, but it is much better to carry on down the far edge towards Llyn Idwal. In a mile or so you will find a series of hummocks and a few cairns at the lowest point of the col. When you come to a small stream, follow it L till it plunges over the cliff. You are now at the top of Twll Du (black hole), more generally called the Devil's Kitchen (VII.ii.f). It is a wonderful prospect, between two huge perpendicular rocks, with Llyn Idwal 1,000 feet below and the Carneddau rising beyond the Nant Ffrancon Pass. A. P. Abraham says it has no equal of its kind in all Britain, and he should know. Your snapshot will resemble thousands taken from the grassy ledge on which you stand, and should be a memorable souvenir of your walks.

The free lance can find a practicable but steep path down to Idwal (VII.ii.f). The top is marked by a biggish cairn further along the cliff. Be very wary of the region in bad weather, although it is a simple route on a clear day. From the foot, the Kitchen looks a gruesome cleft and, in older days, rock climbers were warned off it. Modern techniques, at times aided by rubber soles, now makes it a reasonable climb for experts, in spite of its loose rocks and waterfall. From the base of the Kitchen, Ogwen can be reached by either side of Llyn Idwal.

To return to Llanberis from the Devil's Kitchen, follow the stream southwards to a nearby tarn, Llyn y Cwn, under the shadow of the Glyders (16). The legend goes that fish therein had only one eye. This cannot be proved, since there are none there today. From the lake follow the map, down to Llanberis Pass, with Snowdon before you all the way. You reach the main road, after a final steep drop, about half-a-mile above your starting place (VII.ii.f).

18. ELIDIR BACH AND FAWR, MYNYDD PERFEDD AND CARNEDD Y FILIAST

Today a walk of much variety will complete Section C, with one important exception, Tryfan, that rightly belongs to the Ogwen area (20). To the north of Llanberis, there are two ways to the top of the slate heaps, that can only be used by foot passengers. One is given later (VII.ii.g) and the other is now taken.

Follow the road between the two lakes, Llyn Padarn and Llyn Peris, noting the grim tower of Dolbadarn Castle R and the busy lower network of the quarries along the shores of the lakes. Near the hospital, take a path R winding up through the woods, resembling an alpine way, since it mounts amid pines, with fine views between the trunks. Above the woods bear R and find an open level, with a main road, entrances to quarries and a hamlet with a bus service (VII.ii.g). This is Dinorwic, some seven miles from the Port of that name on the Menai Straits which is one of the outlets for slates from the local quarries. The area is now rapidly changing with the construction of a pumped storage scheme, but none of the routes are much affected by it.

Above the houses R are more slate heaps and you rise beside them by taking a rough path R near the cottage Post Office, Fachwen. Thread your way upwards over stony grass to the top of Elidir Fach (2,565). Although a recorded peak, this is only a spur of the Fawr, that stands to the east. The crossing to the latter is obvious and easy. When the heaped loose stones that mark the summit are reached, circle round a bit and only climb the last and highest pile, to avoid an unpleasant scramble over the shifting surface of the boulders as far as possible.

Elidir Fawr (3,030) is another mountain with a rounded and a steep side. You have ascended by the former and now have quite a sheer drop before you: it appears like a perfect cone from many points on the Carneddau. While lunching, you have another view of Nant Ffrancon, with recent friends, Foel Goch and Y Garn (17) on the other side of a grassy ridge. The Snowdon Massif looks stern and, in some lights, very distant, while the steepest side of the Carneddau rises over the Ogwen. The name Elidir seems to be that of a north-country Briton, who tried to gatecrash these parts by marrying a Welsh princess, but met a sticky end on the seaward plains when he came over to take possession. The fine lake, Marchlyn Mawr, that almost fills the north side of the cwm, also has its legend to the effect that King Arthur's treasure is buried on its shore.

Be that as it may, you now have to follow a pleasing ridge that circles the lake to Mynydd Perfedd (central mountain) (2,665) and pass on with quite level going to the ultimate peak of the grand ridge that runs all the way from the Glyders to this imposing finish. There are ten cwms in its long length. This last peak is Carnedd Y Filiast (hill of the lady greyhound)

(2,695). This lady is the symbol of Ceridwen, the Welsh goddess of plenty. Today greyhounds are only used in the small poaching industry in these parts.

From this vantage point there is a backing of grimness and a bird's-eye view of the Bethesda slate quarries, the largest in the world. After that the land runs down in fertile sweeps to the Menai Straits and over to Anglesey. Môn Mam Cymru (the Mother of Wales). It is so called from the days when its rich fields grew sustenance for the dwellers in the more sterile hills.

The direct descent to Nant Ffrancon, down the last of the cwms, is very steep, but you can make Bethesda more easily by going north over a last buttress, 1,000 feet below, and then through quarry paths to the town, or pass from the buttress towards Llyn y Mynydd along a stream, to reach a road near some rows of houses with wide strips of land between them—an early case of town planning. The latter is more interesting. From Bethesda buses connect with Bangor.

To return to Llanberis you must aim at Llyn Marchlyn Bach and cross some marshy ground, steering west under the shadow of Elidir Fach, till some crofts are reached. Thence Dinorwic is only a short distance along the road. The drop from Dinorwic to Llanberis can be avoided by swinging to the R when under Elidir Fach and making a bee line for the spire of a church at Ebenezer, the end of the village of Deiniolen. At the village a bus service runs to Caenarvon and, by a change at the end of the lower lake, back to Llanberis.

If you wish to shorten the trip by omitting the last two peaks, there is a simple descent from Elidir Fawr to Nant Peris (17). It is rather a long trek down, but furnishes variety and you have a grand view of Snowdon's bulk the whole way.

CHAPTER SIX

From Capel Curig and Ogwen

"You will be amazed when you get among the mountains. There you will see great cliffs and rocky ridges and tarns nestling in lonely hollows and the valleys far below will seem to belong to another world. It is impossible to describe the spirit of the mountains, but you will feel its spell as soon as you get among them."

C. F. KIRKUS

CAPEL Curig, the last junction of the passes, is like Llanberis on the edge of Snowdonia, but it is a very good point on the boundary and makes an excellent springboard. In fact many discerning ramblers make it their regular centre. It is a straggling village with some good hotels and boarding houses, a Youth Hostel and Plas-y-Brenin (see Appendix V). Pen-y-Gwryd is only four miles away and, on the other side, the milder beauties of Betws-y-coed and the Conway Valley are close at hand. The nearest peaks are Moel Siabod and the Southern Carneddau, but other peaks can be tackled without much travelling.

Ogwen, on the other hand, is well in the heart of the mountains. It has a Mountain Centre cum-rescue post, some farmhouses that put up visitors and a very popular Youth Hostel. Several Climbers' Clubs have huts in the region. It is not difficult of access. An excellent main road connects it with the north coast resorts via Bethesda. Since it furnishes plenty of scope for cragsmen it is lively during weekends throughout the year and crowded in the high season. For the walker there are Tryfan, the grim rock circle round Idwal and the steeper side of the Glyders. Across the lake stand the mighty Carneddau.

When Siabod (19) and Tryfan (20) have been dealt with only the Carneddau are left to complete the survey. It is a very considerable "only" since Section D contains 17 summits, six of them over three thousand feet, and occupies some 70 square miles, with only rare tracks and paths. Sheep and a few cattle graze on its lonely stretches and really wild ponies are found there. There are some traces of mining operations and a few of the lakes have been harnessed to the service of man. Apart from the highest parts near Ogwen and some of the foothills on the northside, it is the least visited of any part of Snowdonia. Yet the lover of solitude and wide open spaces will enjoy this expanse of moor and bogland, of lonely cwms and lost lakes, diversified by some impressive cliffs and crags.

19. MOEL SIABOD

Most of the pundits say that the ascent of Moel Siabod (2,860) from Capel Curig is dull, but the pundits are not always right. Try the following route and you will agree that this way up the noble easterly outpost will give as good a day as can be desired.

Cross Pont Cyfyng at the lower end of the village, noting the fine falls below, where the Afon Llugwy tumbles through a mass of huge rocks, turning and twisting between them in a series of noble cascades. Try, however, to choose a day when the water is not too rampant, otherwise you will find the lower reaches rather boggy. Do not take the first by-road R, just over the bridge, but go by the second not far along and ascend a stony farm track that soon rises above the woods. After two small farm houses, leave this track for a straight grassy road leading directly towards a peak ahead which you must not accept as the summit. After about half-a-mile go through a wire fence and rise up a shallow grassy hollow to the skyline.

At the top turn L for a mile of the best sort of ridge walking. It has a little easy scrambling, and at one place a short detour R is needed to dodge a sheer drop. L there is a deep cwm and R a grassy slope that opens out a fine view. The last few hundred yards to the real summit is over grass and the stony top with its big cairn gives yet another varied prospect, more panoramic than from some central peaks.

The Horseshoe semicircle stands out well, a little remote but still imposing.

This is the last eastern peak from which the Glaslyn Vale can be seen. L of it stand the Ffestiniog hills and you will be tempted to walk across to try the long ridge mentioned in (15), but this entails a considerable drop and rise and makes a hard day, ending near Blaenau Ffestiniog. To the L of the ridge, which encircles the widest cwm of all, there is a broad stretch of moorland, leading down to the Lledr Valley, whose sylvan charms are hidden from this point, though the ancient square tower of Dolwyddelen Castle is a prominent landmark. The distant Denbigh Moors carry the eye down to the woods above Betws-y-coed and you can trace the ribbon of the main road up to Capel Curig and, on the other side of the village, another part of the Telford road leading up to Ogwon. Between the two, the Carneddau fill a very wide area and you realise that there is plenty of work to explore them all. L of them, Tryfan is clearly a three peaker from this angle, and the Glyders with their two outliers (16) complete the circle.

Pen-y-Gwryd Hotel is visible under the Glyders and a descent down the long grass slopes to it makes a pleasant afternoon stroll, passing Bwlch-y-main, standing high over yet another hourglass-shaped lake, Llyn Diwaunedd. If going south, bear L above the lake and make a way through rock and then by a rough wooded descent to Llyn Gwynant (VII.ii.d). Among the trees, the west end of the " Ancient Trackway " is not very easy to trace owing to long disuse. Once again you will be near the scene of the Irish 'plane disaster (15). Another descent is over the bogland to Dolwyddelen, with the castle as a landmark and a line of power poles to help.

Probably you will want to return to Capel Curig. Right under the cairn to the east there is a lonely lake, Llyn y Foel, below a drop that looks most fearsome. However if you take a gully with grass ledges at intervals and some boot scratches on the rocks, a little easy scrambling will soon bring you to the ridge above the lake. At a point on its crest, bear L for an easy descent between two sharp cliffs. Pass over the heather to the west shore of the lake. Rest a while in this lonely hollow and wonder how you came down its sheer side so easily. Leaving the lake R, go north-east to " Old Slate Quarry ", a deep pit filled with water. Thence a path leads under a bluff to the wire fence of the upward path.

20. TRYFAN

Tryfan (3,010), a model mountain, always gives a good day's sport, to both walkers and climbers. By its rocky outline, its isolation and its innumerable boot scratches, it can even be tackled in misty weather without much fear of being benighted, but after nightfall it is distinctly dangerous. Its entire make-up is of rock, largely covered by heather and bilberry bushes and it is said to be the only mountain in Wales that cannot be ascended without the use of hand-holds. It has already attracted much attention from other peaks and now its charms shall be described.

The four mainly used ascents are roughly from the four points of the compass. That from the east is the best from Capel Curig. As you come up the main road from that village towards Ogwen, the peak comes into view behind Gallt y Ogof (16) and you see clearly the three tips of its summit, that probably gave rise to its name. Just before Llyn Ogwen, the farmhouse Wern-gof-uchaf stands back from the road L. Turn up a short road to the house. Here cars can be parked (fee)

Tryfan (20), Ogwen falls and the Nant francon from excursion 7(iii)d - Photo E. Emrys Jones

and a welcome cup of tea obtained at the end of the day. As you came up the Pass, you noticed a distinct line, rising from R to L across the face of the mountain dividing it roughly into two halves. This is the Heather Terrace and marks the upward route.

Leave the back of the farm and pass close to some largish slabs of rock L, used by climbers for gymnastics on off days. Then go R by a path over damp ground and rise steeply by some scree to the R end of the Terrace. Once on this the way is clear, but a bit broken by boulders. Even in August you can find ripe bilberries on this part of the hill. You will also see the inevitable sheep and maybe a few goats. The latter have, to use a botanical term, "escaped from cultivation." It is said that they were brought here to crop the steeper ledges, so that the less active sheep should not be tempted into impossible places. Nevertheless this does happen at times. If you see one curled up on a ledge looking very sorry for itself it is wise not to attempt a rescue but report the matter to the nearest farm. Along the Terrace, too, you will pass the base of many recognised climbs and may be able to watch the elaborate technique of assorted rope users.

At last the end of the Terrace is reached. Before you is a miniature duplicate of the whole peak that has been mistaken for the real thing from the other side in misty weather. Turn R up a slope with a bit of grass for a change, until a low wall is reached. Resist the temptation to turn up R before the end of the Terrace, at a point where many scratches are evident. There is a short cut here, but it means some tricky scrambling and novices should not try it alone. Near the stone wall you join the path that comes up from Ogwen and have a very wide view of Nant Ffrancon Pass, with Llyn Bochlwyd (1,806) not far below. It is one of the views, so plentiful in these parts, that call for a halt to impress a memory that will remain when much else is forgotten.

Just over the wall turn R and tackle the boulders that mark the rest of the climb. The path is quite scrappy and the boulders rather large, but luckily they are very firm and the marks of many predecessors will keep you on the right line. Hand and foot will be busy as you haul yourself up, but it is good fun and you will soon reach the southern peak. A fearsome drop will bar your progress and the stark depths of Cwm Tryfan yawn before you. As you work over to the highest point, you will keep well away from the edge if at all affected by vertigo.

At this crest there is no cairn, but instead two solid columns of stone, some six feet above the surrounding tumbled rocks, known as Adam and Eve. They look for all the world like monoliths from far-off Stonehenge. Adam seems a trifle more sturdy than Eve and, if agile, you can get on to his topknot by using a small foothold on his waistline and clawing some shallow wrinkles on his poll. A boost from a friend's shoulder helps to achieve this exalted position. It is a test of a steady head to stand upright on his cranium, while the jump across to Eve's fair brow is a feat best left to cragsmen in rubbers.

As is fitting there is a noble panorama from this most rugged summit: a circle of wild peaks and rolling uplands north, west and south and a long valley vista away to the east.

If centred on Ogwen, you have a somewhat easier way up. Take the path towards Idwal, leaving it soon where there is a sharp turn R and go L in a straight line over rather boggy grass towards a waterfall that tumbles out of the skyline at its lowest point. Just over the crest you reach Llyn Bochlwyd by a path known as the Miner's Track (16). It runs on between Tryfan and Glyder Fach, crossing the shoulder of the latter, where it is more clearly marked, and eventually leads down to Pen-y-Gwryd (16). For Tryfan, you leave it soon after passing Llyn Bochlwyd R and bear L from it towards a patch of brown scree and, near the top of this, is the low wall met with in the previous ascent, so that you finish as already described.

From the south (Penygwryd) take the Miner's Track in reverse (16), using the way to the ridge described as the start up the Glyders and then swinging round the top of Cwm Tryfan, follow path, fairly well marked, either over or round the miniature peak mentioned above, to reach the low wall at the foot of the final scramble. The ascent from the north is the most sporting "walk" up the mountain. Towards the end of Llyn Ogwen going to Capel Curig, halt at the tenth milestone from Bangor. On the R is the Milestone Buttress, a playground for climbers. Crossing the wall at the milestone, circle under the buttress to the L and rise through one of the many tracks through the thick heather to reach the lower end of the Heather Terrace. Then R through the last of the heather and ascend the stony ridge guided by boot marks to the north peak of the mountain. On the way up the "cannon" is passed, a huge projecting rock, clearly visible from Ogwen Cottage. The best tip is to keep well to the R but you cannot avoid some rather exposed places which require a cool head. Do not try this route alone and, for preference, take a companion who has been there before. The last stage presents no great difficulty.

Having dealt with the usual ascents, little need be said

regarding descents. Unless more than a walker, do not try any of the eastern gullies, but make your way back to the wall above Llyn Bochlwyd unless going down the north face. From the wall you have a choice of routes down, by the reverse of the ascents described. Note that, at the lower end of the Heather Terrace, it is easy to regain Ogwen round the foot of the Milestone Buttress and that in clear weather you might try a more direct descent to Ogwen than by the Bochlwyd path.

One final word—Tryfan is unforgiving to the reckless and has had a toll of victims. If treated with due caution, no untoward results need be feared and its rewards are great.

21. CREIGAU GLEISION

The only region left to explore is Section D (the Carneddau). Is is by far the largest area and though not so popular as some others, it will furnish some good and varied excursions. To judge its wide extent and spot the various points from which it can be reached, take an off day and, using car or cycle, circle it on excellent roads. The course runs from Bangor to Capel Curig, down to Betws-y-coed, along the west of the Conway Valley to Conway and back along the coast to Bangor.

It is not easy to split the area into suitable day walks without overlapping, but it will be attempted by clearing off the peaks near Capel Curig, passing on to Ogwen for the big fellows, and completing the rest mainly from the outside edges.

Creigiau Gleision (the blue-green rocks) (2,214) will give an easy day for a start, with more varied scenery than in other parts of the group. Paths from Capel Curig lead up behind the knobby pinnacles of Clogwyn Mawr. One of them, which runs up behind the new church, leaves the knobs L and passes through a wild little valley for a mile, along a small stream. At the highest point turn L, leaving the woods R and drop sharply to Blaen-y-nant farm. Soon there is a good view of the length of Llyn Crafnant, certainly one of the most charming lakes in Wales, with its pastures, wooded slopes and green hills rising behind (VII.iii.a). At one point an inviting cafe has lawns running down to the water. A small chapel, a tiny hamlet and one or two manor houses give an intimate air to this quiet hollow.

Lazy folk, who prefer a fifteen mile drive to a three mile walk, can reach the top end of the lake by driving round from Capel Curig to Trefriw in the Conway Valley and turning L up a delightful, well-wooded vale with a noisy rivulet playing cheerful music as the road rises. When the lake is reached by a monument at the far end, you will certainly be reminded of the "bonny, bonny banks of Loch Lomond," even if the scale is much smaller. You can drive right along the lake to the point where the Capel Curig path joins up and park for the ascent.

Cross a meadow by a farm track near the farmyard and start up the hill to the north. It is largely a matter of trial and error to reach the crest, which is to the L up a stream that wanders through wood and some minor cliffs and then more to the R to the southern end of the Rocks. This is the highest point of a mile-long line of crags and gives a good prospect. The crags run down to the edge of Llyn Cowlyd, a long, narrow lake shut right in at its upper end and opening out lower down where a retaining dam checks the outfall into the Conway Valley, since it is used as a reservoir for works at Dolgarrog. Beyond the valley rises the more cultivated land on the other side of the Conway and on the other side of the lake steep grass slopes lead up to the rolling Carneddau showing the two shapely peaks that will be next visited (22). Westward, over the Ogwen road, are those old friends, the Glyders and their neighbours.

A pleasant way to spend the afternoon is to walk all along the crest and descend to a footpath that passes through woods R to the road up from Trefriw and then R back to the head of the lake. If this is too long a trip, you can go south-west and then south through some broken but interesting country and drop down to the Ogwen road close to Capel Curig. Another variation is to slip down the steep grass slopes to the south end of Llyn Cowlyd to get an impressive view of its whole length. Thence there is a path with a double row of power poles to the main road (22). Near the road is Tal-y-waen, which was the home of one of the first professional guides to rock climbing in the district "Scotty" Dwyer.

If clear weather has blessed your walk, it will not be necessary to underline the caution that the wide open moors of the Carneddau should be avoided in misty weather, even if you are a good map reader and fancy yourself with a compass.

22. PEN LLITHRIG-Y-WRACH AND PEN YR HELGI-DU

These two hills form a graceful outline R as you go up to Ogwen from Capel Curig. If starting from the latter place, leave the highway R at Bronheulog and take a path past Tal-y-waen to the south end of Llyn Cowlyd (21). An avenue of power poles shows part of the way. Just before the lake, take a bee line north up some rather steep slopes to the summit of Pen Llithrig-y-wrach (the slippery hill of the witch) (2,622). If coming from Ogwen, you have a long tramp till you reach half-way between the 12th and 13th milestones, where a track L leads up to Tal-y-braich farm. Take it and, when the farmhouse is passed, pick up a somewhat obscure path beside a small stream that is your guide for a time. Where the path turns R for Cowlyd, leave it and follow the brook. Before long you will meet an odd feature of this long hillside, a leat or wide ditch that runs a winding course of four miles or so across it. Luckily it has several crossing places marked by hand rails that are visible from a distance. Cross the one you meet and then have a long grind up a thousand feet of grass to the top.

This is a good view point. Llyn Cowlyd is right below to the east, with the Blue Rocks (21) looking very jagged on the other side. North is another lake, Eigiau (25), with open country beyond, while on the south the wild north cwms of the core of Snowdonia rise hugely, with Tryfan and the hills beyond its fine cone. Even in haze they look mighty, but they are at their best when snow mantles the giants.

It is very craggy on the far side and Cwm Eigiau, that has to be partly circled, is well protected on three sides. The obvious way to the west is on the edge of these cliffs, so pass down along them over a col and up to the second cairn Pen yr Helgi-du (hill of the black hound) (2,733). Llyn Cowlyd is now out of sight, but the smaller and more romantic Ffynnon Llugwy appears to the west and northwards the widest stretch of the Carneddau is seen.

On the shores of the lake below, there was a sad tragedy, when two young climbers lost their lives on a misty autumn night some years ago. This was mainly due to the callous action of an insane senior who had taken them for a climb on Craig yr Ysfa on an impossible day. The full story can be read in *I Bought a Mountain*. On a sunny day it seems incredible that any danger can lurk in so peaceful a valley, but the scene is different when clouds roll down and mist fills its lonely hollows.

Do not leave Helgi without going out a little to the north-west to see the fierce mass of Craig yr Ysfa, where many climbers, who do not mind a long tramp to their base, come to exercise their talent. Indeed you will want to linger for a long time to absorb the beauties of the wide solitudes of this edge of the Carneddau.

When the time comes to depart, you have a wide choice of descents. If on a tour, you can drop back to the col and try Traverse No. 9, right over to the Conway Valley. The walk due south, down a wide, gentle grass slope, with the far side of the Ogwen Valley before you all the way, is a very satisfying end to the day. After the first mile there is some bogland, but a track leading to a bridge over the leat, a little to the R, avoids some of it. Make a bee line for the road when you have crossed the leat and you will come out at the Helyg Hut, close to the starting place from Ogwen.

With time in hand, you can keep along the north-west ridge to explore the upper parts of Craig yr Ysfa. It is a lofty walk and one or two points in it are almost worthy to be listed as peaks. From one of them, Pen y Waenwen, it is only a half-mile or so to the summit of Carnedd Llywelyn, the nearest rival to Snowdon, but that is reserved for another skyline (23). So, from this slight angle, circle round the cwm L on the 2,500 contour to save a sharp drop and then follow any of the rivulets that run down to supply Llyn Ogwen. If you take the most westerly of them, make a detour to inspect the lofty little Ffynnon Lloer, a haunt of anglers. You should meet the road somewhere near the east end of Ogwen lake.

Between these two southward descents there is another that can be taken from any point on the ridge. Scramble down steep slopes to shore of Ffynnon Llugwy, that may tempt you to a dip in sultry weather. Leaving it on your R, you will trace some sort of a path that will lead you back to the Climbers' Hut at Helyg on the main road.

23. PEN-YR-OLE-WEN, CARNEDD DAFYDD, CARNEDD LLYWELYN AND YR ELEN

The heading looks formidable. To tackle four peaks in the three thousand class in one trip seems a hard day's work. It certainly is stiff, but if you have done the Horseshoe (6), with its switchbacks and scramblings, you will manage this longer distance, since the going is much easier after the first pull up. As on the Glyders (16) you will spend a long time on one of the highest plateaux south of the border.

Start from the west end of Llyn Ogwen, near the popular Falls. Leave the road over a low wall and edge round the lake a bit, between the water R and a rock face L. Then, while you are fresh, tackle the stiffest part of the climb. The rise is well over two thousand feet in a mile. Though steep, the going is not too difficult and some sort of a path exists here and there, since the route is used a good deal. It is as well to bear to the R for the easiest gradient; in any case the cliffs will hold you off the L. You will puff and blow a bit when you reach the cairn on Pen-yr-Ole-wen (the hill of the white light) (3,211) and a longish rest will be well rewarded in its pure air.

Pen-yr-Ole-Wen (23) from the path above Llyn Idwal - Photo E. Emrys Jones

You will agree with connoisseurs who say that it gives the finest view on the Carneddau. The grimmest cwm in Wales is right opposite, beyond the sheer drop of the Pass. Circling Llyn Idwal stand Tryfan (20), the precipitous sides of the Glyders (16), a line of cliffs with the black Devil's Kitchen in the middle, the sharpest sides of Y Garn and Foel Goch (17), Elidir Fawr (18), a perfect cone from this side, and finally the hills running down to Bethesda. The catalogue is familiar, but from this point the outlines are quite new. Indeed, the whole day gives you entrancing all-round vistas.

It is a fairly wide ridge that leads northward for a mile to Carnedd Dafydd (3,427), with impressive cwms on either side. On the R is the hollow described in (22) with the triangular tarn, Ffynnon Lloer (moon fountain), on the near side and Ffynnon Llugwy under the cliffs at the far edge. On the L is a steep drop to Nant Ffrancon and beyond, a more gentle slope down to Bethesda. This last marks a way out available from almost every point of these heights. From the broad brow of Dafydd yet another cwm comes into sight, Cwm Llafar (the valley of sound). It seems to have got its name from the straight river that runs through its long and rather dull extent. However it will steer you right down to Bethesda in case of need.

The ridge passes on, widening out to a stony plateau, to Dafydd's twin brother Carnedd Llywelyn (3,485) only a few feet lower than Snowdon itself. As you go over, keep well to the L to look down the Ysgolion Dduon (black ladders), cliffs sometimes used by rock climbers, although the rocks are not so clean and hard as those on the other side of the valley.

The brothers are very much alike, except that the higher is the meeting place of four ridges, whereas Dafydd has only two. After the Black Ladders, the well marked path leaves Craig Llugwy (3,185), too flat to be listed, on the R and bears L along a narrow ridge. This opens out into a stony waste rising to the summit. Some circular stone walls near the top give shelter on windy days.

A short account of the four ridges that meet at this point is now given, since each of them affords a way of access to the summit. The one south-west from the top has just been traversed; the south-east ridge goes to Pen yr Helgi-du (22) in about a mile; that to the north-east leads to Foel Grach (24) and is flat and wide; while north-west links up with Yr Elen. With the exception of the second, all the peaks at the end of these arms exceed three thousand feet. Yet so wide is the tableland, that there is less sense of being on high than on the switchback of the Horseshoe (6). The scene, too, is as vast as the platform from which you view it.

Now is the time to bag Yr Elen (3,152), by an amusing little down and up walk along the north-west arm. Near the top, the sharp edge R juts out from the grassy slopes L like dragon's teeth. The tiny tarn at the bottom of the cliffs adds to their grimness (24).

It is time to end this day on the central core of the Carneddau. From Yr Elen there is a three-mile easy stroll down to Bethesda on the north side of Cwm Llafar or you can go back to Llywelyn and use either of the other ridges. That to Foel Grach (24) will land you at far off Aber at a late hour. The Helgi ridge is also a long one (22), so try going back to Craig Llugwy (see above). From this point slant across, under the shadow of the day's first peak. This brings you out at the far end of Llyn Ogwen as described in the last walk. In any case your legs will ache at the end of the day.

24. BERA MAWR, GYRN WIGAU, YR ARYG, FOEL GRACH, FOEL FRAS AND LLWYTMOR

As stated, the final area of the Carneddau will mainly be approached from the outside edges. The district not yet visited is roughly a rectangle dotted with peaks, with one lone sentinel outside it. Many ramblers try a long cross-country course from Aber or Llanfairfechan to Ogwen and find it an entertaining, though rather tiring pull. They are bound to miss one or two peaks before they reach the giants (23), so today, to fulfil the idea of calling on every cairn, a circular trip will be taken, based on Aber.

Go inland from the main road along the north coast at Aber. If using a vehicle, park it at the bridge a short mile up the valley. If you go further up the by-road, over the bridge, you miss the best starting place. For a further mile or so, follow a pleasantly wooded path, used by hundreds that call a walk to Aber Falls a good day's work. Having duly admired the highest waterfall in Wales, you have to get out of a kind of cul de sac. The quickest way is to step over the fence L and scramble up the edge of some scree through rocks and bushes till you reach a sketchy path that bears R. This will bring you to the top of the Falls, round an awkward corner or two. Keeping the Afon Goch R, make your way upstream into a fine amphitheatre. Here is a favoured spot of the small wild ponies that live on these hills. They are not too shy of humans and gipsies occasionally catch them and break them in. Their breeding place is near the tiny tarn under Yr Elen (23), which has a Welsh name, Ffynnon Caseg, meaning Mare's Well.

The first skyline is R but do not cross the river and ascend until a stone sheep fold is passed in the valley. After this there is an easy grass slope up the flank of Bera Mawr (2,588) with its stony crest, or rather, plateau. From it you see the vast quarries of Bethesda below and far-off view of the line of impressive peaks on the other side of Nant Ffrancon.

To bag all the hills, go over by the stone heap marked Drosgl on the map, to reach Gyrn Wigau (2,019), which is just a slightly crested moor. By the way, if Aber is not a suitable starting point, it is easy to commence the hills at this minor one, by going up behind the church in the town of Bethesda, turning L beside a stream and follow a by-road to the ultimate farm, Parc, once the home of a Welsh poet. Thence the hill rises ahead and the going is good over grass. But this route means a long trek back to Llwytmor.

Whether from Bera or Wigau, it is a pull across to Yr Aryg (2,876), another grass ridge with stony patches. Now the higher Carneddau come into sight and you will enjoy the down and up mile over to Foel Grach (3,196) which is high enough to look Llywelyn (23), another mile away, in the face. The cwm under Yr Elen, with its dragon's teeth, also makes a fine show just opposite. A cubby hole in the summit cairn is a suitable place for lunch. The view north and west is somewhat uniform aspect of rounded hills, giving an impression of spaciousness.

If you are going on to Ogwen, a wide ridge will take you in twenty minutes to Llywelyn (23) but, to collect more scalps on the way back to Aber, there is a long walk northwards over to Foel Fras (3,092). On the way there it is worth while making a detour R to look down a cliff face to the loneliest lakes of all, Melynllyn and Llyn Dulyn (the yellow and black lakes) (25). Above them is the gentler side of Craig Eigiau (25). Foel Fras is positively the last of the three-thousanders, the final goal of those hardy souls who try to visit all fourteen of them in record time. It has a long, flat top with traces of an ancient wall and its sides are stony. North-west is the round top of Drum (25), on a sweep that is too far for today, so make your way over to Llwytmor (2,750), the last cairn on this long round.

Here you have a vision of the whole of Conway Bay and a corner of Anglesey, with Puffin Island hanging on its tail over the Lavan Sands. Far off the Great Orme stands boldly out to sea. On the east, the Conway Valley, more or less visible all day, shows its course winding inland, with its tidal waters reaching nearly to Llanwrst. This final peak has a stony top, with typical upended shafts of slaty rock.

Westwards the Afon Goch winds down to the Falls and you make your way down to the stream and along to the top of them, through the grass and bilberry bushes. When you reach the path used on the upward way, follow it round to the top of the scree. You can slide down this or follow the upper path right down to the bridge at Aber. You will be grateful for the shade of the woods on the way back, since you should only try this round on a sunny day.

25. CRAIG EIGIAU, PEN Y CASTELL AND DRUM

It will be noted that only four minor Carneddau remain to be visited. These are rather remote from the through highways and, like those in the last trip, they will be tackled from the outside. For three of them there is a good base in the Conway Valley. It is a moorland walk after the first rise, giving a view of some of the Ogwen friends from the far side and a prospect of the Conway Valley on your return.

If you have a taste for Alpine motoring, take your car to Tal-y-Bont on the west side of the Conway Valley and turn up the road on the south side of the bridge in the hamlet. You will soon be in low gear as you climb, and you will meet some gradients and hairpin bends equal to anything in Switzerland in the narrow road with its rough surface. In a long mile the track levels out a bit and there is a farmhouse on the right. If you value your tyres, you will be well advised to park here. Follow on the same by-road for about two miles, where it crosses a wide brown moor. Over on the R some rocks show up, that mark the end of a ridge. This is your objective and you choose the best path across the sedges towards them. For firmer ground do not take off R too soon. The footpaths shown on the map are not easily found, but they may help you, if you do not mind a bit of a detour.

You come out at the north end of Llyn Eigiau, where a small dyke leads to a tunnel, and, after this, the going is drier. Work a slant across the grass on the west side of the lake to hit the top of the ridge where the rocks begin. Like Creigiau Gleision, the hill is a jumble of rocks extending some distance and the highest point is Craig Eigiau (2,390). The actual summit is above the centre of the lake and commands a view of the major Carneddau (23) that make a stern circle of rock to the south, with Pen Llithrig (22), gracefully aloof at the end of them. Westwards are the sheer cliffs over the almost hidden lakes, Dulyn and Melynllyn (24). If making for Ogwen, you can work across near the latter to reach the top of Craig yr Ysfa (22) and proceed by routes described earlier. Otherwise set a course due north when you have finished pottering among these uplands. Make your way towards twin rocks across a long valley. The easy descent is by a wall for some distance and then towards a glimpse of water in the course of the Afon Dulyn. Again there is some unavoidable bogland. Sheeptracks should help you across for the animals pass in a single file over wet ground and make a firmer path that sometimes proceeds in a desired direction. There is a minor problem in crossing the stream, but once over, it is an easy rise to Pen y Castell (2,035). Again you have a bunch of rocks to mark the top and can find a dry, if hard, seat to view "the landscape o'er." You will be a little nearer the wide sweep of the Conway Valley and notice that Tal y Fan (26) is a long ridge away to the north.

It is almost a level mile over to Drum ridge (2,529), with one bit of a rise halfway over. Drum is about the most featureless of all the hills, but as you sit on its bald top you will be once more impressed at the extent of the Carneddau. Drosgl away to the north, also a point used by the ordnance surveyors, is not listed, as it has no worthy crest.

As to the homeward path, if not tied to a base, it is pleasant to walk down to Llyn Anafon, a tarn a thousand feet below, and follow its emerging stream to the woods of Aber. Or you can go over the moors by Drosgl to Llanfairfechan (26), ending down a smaller stream. Otherwise you must retrace your steps, skirt Pen y Castell on its south side to find your way back to base. Make towards a deserted small farm. Below it is a leat that can be crossed by a bridge. The next point is the R end of a belt of small trees marking the course of the Afon Dulyn. In the woods, a riverside path leads L to some rough stepping stones close to a farm called "Rowlyn". A track from the farm above the stones leads back to the upward road. You meet it at the larger farm where you were advised to park the car.

26. TAL Y FAN

Tal y Fan (2,001), just qualifying for the list, is a solitary outpost away to the north-east, giving a very good half day. Its cairn is on the eastern edge of the ridge that forms its skyline. From the main road at Llanfairfechan, turn inland, pass the Post Office and ascend R and then L till you cross a small bridge and come to a point where the road meets a cross one, with a gate L. The angle gives a good parking place. The route goes L through the gate, overlooking some pretty tea-gardens outside a honeysuckled cottage and leads upwards near a stream for some distance. Cross a cement bridge and follow the track.

If you want a direct ascent, take the L stream soon after this, rounding the steep Dinas, since the rough grassy cone you see before you is not the summit, which lies further back to the L, nearer the distinctive top of the quarry at Penmaenmawr. But it makes a more pleasing walk to follow the R brook, Afon Ddu, for a while, till a faint track across a field L leads to a gate in a stone wall. After this take a bee line over marshy ground to the hill ahead. Its grassy ascent is drier and on the top (1,963), there is a wall that runs along L down and up to the two rocky peaks of Tal y Fan, with a path along its north side, making for easy progress.

You have turned your back on the rolling spaces of the Carneddau but face Conway Bay. On this last crest you will rest at the cairn to see the view from the ultimate buttress of Snowdonia. It gives you the Vale of Conway, the Sychnant Pass, the Great Orme and a wide ocean expanse, as well as the vast hills behind that fill the southern horizon.

There are pleasant ways down to the east and north, either to the pretty hamlet of Roe Wen (Y.H.) in the Conway Valley, or over to the Druid's Circle, a prehistoric monument above Penmaenmawr. To return to your starting point, however, make for a V-shaped cut with the rocky dome of the Dinas R and the yellow side of a small quarry L. It is a long and often damp stretch across to it. Here and there over the upland are paths and tracks, but they often confuse. In clear weather your eye is the best guide. As is often said, the Carneddau are not pleasant in mists and certainly they are more enjoyable in dry seasons.

CHAPTER SEVEN

Some lower walks and traverses

> **"There is an evanescent charm about the British hills, due in a part to the changes of colour with the seasons, but more strongly influenced by the atmosphere which affects the distances and lends mystery to the scene."**
>
> W. A. POUCHER

IT may be that some readers are not equal to the somewhat lofty excursions that have been described, and even the hardiest may like an off day now and then. Therefore these few notes on attractive trips that do not entail much high work, are given more or less as samples. Some of them are a bit stiff, however, and the contours on the map should be consulted before sampling them. The walks are not all circular and some finish a long way from the starting place when they cross a bwlch or pass. But it is easier in most cases to regain a main road and pick up a bus if overtaken by weariness or bad weather, than when on higher ground. Cross references are given when the route has been mentioned earlier. Short walks described in the many local guide books are not included, nor those along the north coast.

i. BEDDGELERT AND THE SOUTH

(a) The Tremadoc Cliffs

The architecture of the foothills south of Snowdon is more graceful than that of the bulky Carneddau on the other side, and so they furnish some varied strolls. A start will be made by visiting a series of rocky waves that seem poised to break over into the village of Tremadoc. On the road down to it you will see that at times they do so break, as traces of a recent fall can be seen on the road from Beddgelert about half-a-mile short of Tremadoc. To reach the top of these imposing cliffs, take a track at the back of a laundry, to reach the outbuildings of Tan-y-rallt, a mansion once occupied by Mr. Maddocks, who built the Embankment over the Traeth, and so created the sites for Portmadoc and Tremadoc, both towns of comparatively recent origin. Shelley once stayed in the house. He was not popular in the district, owing to his habit of shooting suffering sheep.

There is a choice of routes at the back of the mansion. By following a farm road away from it, you can reach the outer wave, soon turning L up a wall to its edge. A pleasant mile or so on good turf will take you switchbacking along, high over the roofs of the houses to an end in rocks on a minor peak (891). A rather steep drop to the Caernarvon-Portmadoc road allows you to return to Tremadoc by a quiet by-road inside the main one. From the peak a variation is to turn inland and go over open country up to the higher second line of cliffs with a much rougher crest, and to reach Tan-y-rallt by the little lost lake of Cwmbach. This tarn is often choked by weeds in dry weather, but it has an interesting flora. Keep it on the L and at its end a path leads back to the mansion.

Another perhaps better route is to leave Tan-y-rallt by this path, starting over a small stone stile turning R through a wood by a stream, till you come to some steps with a rail to assist you. This was the crofters' short cut to the market, but now many of the smallholdings are deserted and cottage ruins dot the uplands. Passing between some high stones, turn R to a grassy space, for a grand view of the Glaslyn Vale and an ideal spot for a picnic. A variety of routes now opens out. After some small cliffs, turn L by a deserted farmhouse for a path to the lake already mentioned. Or keep R as close to the cliffs as you can, for a way down to the village of Prenteg on the Beddgelert road.

A longer way is to cross the moor to the third wave of cliffs, with here and there a farm track to help. The last farm is Tai-cochion, now deserted. Thence the way must be picked out under the foot of Moel Ddu by some woods and going L to a couple of tiny tarns, Llyn Oerddwr (Cold Water), whence faint paths lead down to Aberglaslyn or go on to Beddgelert. The double summit of Moel Ddu (1,811) can be included. You are warned that this is quite hard going, but reminded that at many points it is possible to drop down to the main road R. In any case a visit to this little-known tract of country will always furnish new possibilities and unusual scenes.

(b) Moel y Gest

From the Tremadoc Cliffs and indeed from most of the southern heights, you saw to the south a ridged peak, the very last outpost of Snowdonia in this direction. It is Moel y Gest (861), a pocket mountain, standing watch and ward over Cardigan Bay. It is a jolly little hill for novices as it contains all aspects of hill walking in miniature, and there is a surprising amount of space to explore on its long summit, apart from the excellent views, finer than those of many a two-thousander. There is a way up from the north, but a visit can be combined with a day by the sea if you drive through Portmadoc and turn R at the Town Hall and again R at the top of the hill beyond, to reach the scattered hamlet of Morfabychan, with a golf course, odd cottages, bungalows a rash of caravans, and a fine shallow sandy shore. One of the best ways up the hill is by the path R, just before you drop down to the village; it is marked by a signpost " Public Footpath ". This path runs over some fields and you soon leave it R and scramble up between the cliffs to reach the centre of the ridge.

If you turn L on its crest, you will come to its western tip, with a wide sea view, Criccieth Castle on its grassy mound and Lleyn stretching beyond, as well as a varied aspect of the south side of Snowdonia. Some traces of prehistoric man remain and it is said that some rounded pebbles here were ammunition dumps for the users of slings. An amusing hour can be spent exploring the long ridge. On the north side there is an old granite quarry where ravens nest, that can be visited, but care is needed in going along the top side of it. It is easy to descend from any part of the crest, but there are more paths on the east side than on the west.

(c) Cwm-y-stradllyn

There are two interesting traverses to the south from Beddgelert and Rhyd-ddu that are better done from the outside inwards, if only for the view that greets you when the top of the col is reached. The first, up the wide cwm containing Llyn Cwm-y-stradllyn, can be done from Tremadoc (a) by skirting between the outer and second wave of cliffs and bearing R to Llyn Du. Farm paths lead at length to the east side of the lake and then R up to the ridge for the two tarns in (a).

By going two miles up the Caernarvon road from Tremadoc you find a turning R, that can be used by cars as far as the lake. On the way there is the shell of an old building that looks like a ruined abbey, but is actually the remains of a slate mill, deserted since the rash of red tiles spread over the land in place of the hodden grey that used to cover all roofs. A big water scheme has been developed in this valley. Cars should be parked near Tyddyn-mawr and a track followed to Plasllyn, a deserted house in a copse (no longer a Y.H.). Pass on round under the old quarry and rise to the skyline. Here you see Beddgelert right below and the giants fill a noble horizon. From the quarry there is a way up Moel Hebog (7). If on a traverse drop directly towards Beddgelert. The paths are not clear, but one to the R, near the first farm reached, ends by a steep and long-neglected one through woods that comes out very close to Aber Glaslyn Bridge.

(d) Pennant Valley

The second traverse, a very good one, is not easy to start from the south, but it is better to take the awkward journey in the morning and finish at the inner point, than to end far from home. The Caernarvon bus from Portmadoc must be left just past the wool factory at the signpost Cwm Pennant. At once you discover why the Valley (7 and 8) is so famous and all the way the variety of the scene makes it a worthwhile outing.

After the first old stone bridge, a tower is seen on a hillock R, a little off the road. It can be climbed for a wide prospect, but only with extreme care. It is reputed to have been built by an old squire for his student sons, a fitting spot for meditation. Hard by are the ruins of his mansion, Brynkir Hall. Just before the neglected drive to it, the road turns L and, after another bridge, sharp R and then meanders on by a small church, another old bridge, a tiny disused school and over a hill to a chapel. From the last there is a way R over a col and down to Beddgelert (7). This is a stiffish pull and you should bear L up the main valley, shadowed by hills until the road peters out into a path.

There seems no easy way through the hills ahead, but if you mount R over grass, you will come to the relics of a quarry and a row of ruined huts. Thence a path helps you, under the beetling cliffs of Moel Lefn (7), to the top of the rise for a side view of Snowdon and a chance of seeing the small train puffing up or sliding down. On the slopes below, much timber was cut in the two wars, but now the Forestry Commission is repairing the damage. The path branches, one leg going R to Beddgelert (7), and the other L, by Llyn y Gader, to Rhyd-ddu both now filled with plantations of pines. Few ten-mile walks equal this one.

(e) Under Snowdon

A rather strenuous round can be made under the shadow of Snowdon itself by taking the lower parts of (4) and (1). Start up the Watkin Path, past the Chalet and the pleasing waterfalls till the Gladstone Rock is reached. A little beyond, at some ruined quarry huts, bear L from the path and go westward up to the skyline—a longish pull. Here are more old quarries and a couple of tarns (1,500). A quarry track leads down to Rhyd-ddu (1) or you can reach Beddgelert under Yr Aran (11) and Craig Wen by a footpath that seems to have disappeared.

(f) Nantmor Vale

From Beddgelert take the first part of the route up Cnicht (13). When the chapel is reached, keep on down the road R in a narrow valley, with a stream for company all the way. In two miles you will pass, Cae Ddafydd, once one of the most picturesque Youth Hostels in Wales, where American engineers trained during the last war. Half-a-mile beyond it, leave the stream by turning R over a bridge and follow a wooded lane to Nantmor village and then turn R at the main road for Aber Glaslyn Bridge. The whole round is ten miles and, by detours at the start and finish, can be done by car, but the motorist misses half the beauty of a fine round.

(g) Moel Dyniewyd (1254)

There is an inner circle walk within the confines of (f), overlooked by mountains on every side. It is better to start the walk near Nantmor than by the steep path behind the Beddgelert church, though that is a good way off the hill.

A little beyond the east side of Aberglaslyn Bridge is a National Trust parking place R. On the opposite side of the road go through a gate and under the disused railway track. Leaving the rusty remains of quarry workings L, find a path by a stream upwards by some old pylons to reach yet another disused quarry. When this is passed bear R of a yellow mark on the hill to reach the top on that side.

The rest on the cairn is rewarding since you have much to see. Fine peaks are all around you and Llyn Dinas and Nantmor Vale right below. You can explore the moor around in many directions. One ridge leads above the copper mines till you are right on top of Beddgelert and can drop down to it, by the path mentioned, or follow on till above the sheer cliffs of Aberglaslyn and work down behind them to the car park. From the bridge, the Fisherman's Path takes you back to Beddgelert, avoiding the main road.

(h) Aberglaslyn to Tan-y-bwlch

This "three star" walk has been mentioned in (14). It is said to be a Roman road, but it is not a very straight one. Follow the tail of (f) from Aberglaslyn to the bridge below the Youth Hostel, but then cross straight over the road, up a rough track that winds over wild country to the village of Croesor, under Cnicht (13). The by-road now rises and passes below the Moelwyns (14), by a lonely farm or two and over a hummocky plain to Tan-y-bwlch Station (14).

All the way the views have been good and here a climax is reached. There is a path down to Llyn Mair and then a road down to the Oakley Arms, whence you can return by a couple of bus rides via Portmadoc. Altogether a most entertaining eight miles.

ii. PEN-Y-PASS, PEN-Y-GWRYD AND LLANBERIS

(a) Beddgelert to Pen-y-pass

In proceeding from Beddgelert to higher regions, it is as

well to walk up, if you can solve the problems of baggage, that bugbear of all travellers. In his *Tours in Wales* (Vol. II), Pennant has a good deal to say about this area, terming it, "the most beautiful vale in Snowdonia." If interested in old legends and times, you should read his book. Pennant was no mean rambler, Snowdon, the Glyders and Cwm Tryfan were among his conquests in days when roads were primitive and few paths helped the walker.

Take the opening stage of (13) to Llyn Dinas and, since the former bridge at the south side of the lake has gone, keep close to its eastern shore and over some meadows till you reach the cement bridge that leads back to the main road. Turn R and soon after the start of the Watkin Path (4) and a stone bridge, you will have a fine profile of Snowdon L up a narrow cwm. Half-a-mile further along the road, just before some cottages L, look out for a small gap in the wall. Go through it and over a field, to see one of the finest rough stone bridges in the country. Lately it has been rather spoilt by repairs, after damage by floods. An old broken track on the far side of Llyn Gwynant can be used, but it is very rough, so go back to the road again and proceed to the end of the lake. Where the road rises, take a by-road L to pass up the valley of Cwm Dyli. This lower road is practicable for cars and cycles, but the rise at the end is severe.

It is pleasant up the dale, with the infant Glaslyn running down by green pastures and farmhouses. Here Pennant shared curds and whey with the haymakers in their hafod-ty or summer house. Like the Swiss, the old-time Welsh farmer only occupied the upper pastures in the summer time, going lower down in the cold weather. After his meal Pennant climbed up the waterfall to Llyn Llydaw (b).

For Pen-y-Gwryd stick to the by-road till it rejoins the main one not far from the hotel. For Pen-y-pass, turn down to the Power Station and follow a line of poles and a small brook up steep grass. If you wish to emulate old Pennant, cross the bridge to the Power Station and follow the directions of (b). The small cottage near the Power Station is the home of the ladies of the Pinnacle Club.

(b) Cwm Dyli and Llydaw

Both Pen-y-Gwryd and Pen-y-pass stands very high and you are tempted to try something big from such convenient bases, so that only a few hints are needed about shorter trips. You stoop to conquer by going down the steep road to the Power Station in Cwm Dyli (a) and then scrambling up, not far from its ugly black iron pipes, by the side of a waterfall that is charming as a close-up, though its volume was greatly reduced early this century when the waters of Llyn Llydaw were tapped to supply the slate quarries with electric current.

At the top of the fall there is a wide space of open country which you may cross by a faint path made by lady climbers on their way to Lliwedd. In a mile you reach Llydaw, admired from on high in early walks (6). There is a good track back to Pen-y-pass from the lake end circling Llyn Teyrn, with its group of roofless quarrymen's cottages. Up to 1914, on Saturdays, you could meet dozens of miners skipping over the cols to the lowlands to spend their Sundays in their favourite chapels, after a week's work in the copper mines.

Across the narrow part of the larger lake, too, you will notice a causeway. Since the pipe line was constructed, it is sometimes under water, but if dry, it makes a pleasant variation to cross it, mount the hill on the far side R, and come down almost on the roof of Pen-y-pass.

For longer extensions you can circle the lake, under the stern cliffs of Lliwedd, or even mount from its far end a stony five hundred feet to the shores of Glaslyn, to return by the lower half of the Pyg Track (5). By the way, there is a cautionary tale about the causeway. In 1911, a climber returning over it in a gale was blown off and drowned in the lake, so watch your step in a high wind.

(c) Cwm-y-Ffynnon

A mild little outing can be made to the shores of Llyn Cwm-y-Ffynnon, tucked away out of sight within a quarter of a mile of the main road. Follow the stream L (16) just behind Pen-y-Gwryd, to reach the lake in a mile or so. Circle its northern side and come down after a rise, to Pen-y-pass. Do not try to drop into Llanberis Pass too soon, but keep up to pass a huge boulder precariously perched on the edge of the hillside, that has been listed as a natural wonder. From the lake you can explore the top of Moel Berfedd (1,571) a fine viewpoint that is seldom visited. This cwm figures in the last chapter of *I Bought a Mountain*, when its author extended his holding to include this lonely valley.

(d) The Slopes of Siabod

The big moorland rising up from Pen-y-Gwryd to Siabod (19) is not very inviting, but it gives a pleasant stroll on a clear evening. The sunset over Snowdon will live in your memory. Leave the artificial lake in front of the hotel on the L as you go up. Not long ago this attractive tarn was boggy land, but Mr. Lockwood, then landlord of the hotel and later well-known resident, built a strategic dam to create, not only a welcome break in the monotony, but some occupation for anglers.

As you rise you have a good view of Capel Curig lakes down the valley. On meeting a brook, turn up it for the small rise to Cefn y Cerig (1,363), whence you get a noble prospect to the west. Now you can go over to Y Cribau (1,938) or drop down to the double lake Llyn Diwaunedd (19) in a lost hollow, to follow the power lines R, north of the latter peak back to the main road. In the opposite direction the lines will give a rough guide over to Roman Bridge with its Youth Hostel.

For the benefit of any walkers who project a walk from Gwynant to Dolwyddelen, it may be noted that a start can be made from the main road where it widens through a gate a mile above Llyn Gwynant. The path is obscure at first through woods, but if you keep well R away from the stream you come out by some sheep folds to a wire fence. At a gate in it the path marked " Ancient Trackway " on the map becomes clear. At the top of the woods, keep a cubical rock with grass on its top on the R. It was R of this path that the Irish 'plane crashed.

* * *

The next walks are based on Llanberis, but note that the Miners' Track from Pen-y-Gwryd to Ogwen is dealt with in (16 and iii.e) and that Cwm Glas can be approached by dropping down from Pen-y-pass.

(e) Cwm Glas

This almost unique valley affords you more chances of losing your way than any other, it deserves priority in your list, albeit the walk is quite strenuous. At the eleventh mile-stone from Caernarvon, two miles down the Pass, leave the main road R and cross a cement bridge near Blaen y Nant Farm with a Climbing Club hut close by. Before you rises a semicircle of cliffs that seems difficult to tackle without ropes. But it can be done. Keep R up the stream, crossing it where it divides, noting the faint path used by climbers on their way to the Parson's Nose. On the flat. where the ground is boggy, rest a while. On the small rock face in front of you, that has water-falls on either side, you will see on the top a boulder that has all the appearance of a squat toad.

Either side of this cliff will give a reasonable ascent, the one R landing you well into the far side of the cwm. Keep fairly near the stream, with boot scratches to guide, till over the top you come to a tiny tarn that just secures a special marking on the map. It sparkles in a rocky hollow dominated by the imposing rock mass of the Parson's Nose (Clogwyn y

Person, on the map). Here hundreds of rock climbers have had a first lesson in their art. Crib y Ddysgl (2 and 6) rears its cliffs R, with a route up Snowdon well out on that side.

To complete the cwm, follow the brook to the larger lake, just round the corner and at a lower level. Here a pause is needed to absorb the finest close-up of Crib Goch and its Pinnacles.

On a recent Boxing Day, it was amusing to scan the ridge with field glasses and pick out the ramblers crossing it. A few went with fearless upright stance, but most of them used the footholds down on the other side, fondling the icy crest with chilly fingers, so that their heads bobbed along the sky-line. There is a saucer-like extension to the cwm L, ending in the jutting mass of rock glowering down the Pass and called Dinas Mot. You can reach Pen-y-pass by a cairned route, by making for the lower edge of the scree between Dinas Mot and the main peaks, till you join the Pyg Track (5) near Bwlch Moch.

As you rest by Llyn Glas, there is another tempting variation. To the R of the Pinnacles, you see a line of stones and scree running up to the col between Crib Goch and Crib y Ddysgl. If you have an hour to spare, this is certainly worth climbing to renew your acquaintance with the Horseshoe (6) at the col, Bwlch Goch, with its fine southerly prospect. Many variations arise from this central point. Due south by steep grass or scree, you can get down to the Copper Mines (5) and by skirting Llyn Glaslyn traverse to Beddgelert over the Gribin (6). R or L from the col you can do Snowdon or Crib Goch.

If, however, you are based on the milestone, slide back down to Llyn Glas and, keeping fairly close under Dinas Mot, come out on the other side of the toad rock, to end a jolly day by the upward path.

(f) The Top of the Devil's Kitchen

It is a moot point whether you can call a walk that rises to over two thousand feet a lower one, but a good outing can be had by combining the start and finish of (17) in reverse. Leave the main road past Nant Peris at the point "390" on the map and pass up a track to a small croft or two to find a path that keeps near the middle of the three branches of the Afon Las. The start, through a few scrubby hawthorn bushes, is quite steep and the path rather vague, but bear L by the first cliffs.

On the skyline things are easier, the rise is more gradual and there are many cairns along cwm Cneifio following the main stream that leads over boggy land right up Llyn y Cwn

(16, 17). Near the lake there is a queer jumble or rocky hummocks and small bogs that is confusing. To reach the famous viewpoint, follow the small stream from the lake till you come to its vertical cliffs. You can take your snapshot from a convenient grassy hollow. This is also a good spot for lunch.

This central col offers many possibilities. From the largest cairn a steep path runs down to Ogwen (17), and well round to the R rises the edge of the Nameless Cwm, while above the lake is the scree up to Glyder Fawr. But this is a milder trip and you can get back on a different route by skirting Y Garn, the mountain to the north, till you see the hamlet of Nant Peris straight below and then make for it, admiring the grand view of Snowdon across the valley (17).

(g) The Zigzags

This is an amusing after-dinner stroll from Llanberis. Take the road between the twin lakes (18) and, close to the main gate to the quarries R, there is a narrow opening on the L of it. Turn up it for the longest semi-stairway in Wales, beating even the Roman Steps in continuity. It threads it way to and fro, right up through the great mass of waste slate that marks the north side of Llyn Peris. The sides are so high that you have to insert a toe in a crevice and hop up to mark your progress. At length you reach more open country, among small trees and can see where you are.

Out of the woods, there is a rather sunless house R and some cottages under another terrific pile of waste. Then by a quarry entrance, you reach the hamlet of Dinorwic (18) and Fachwen Post Office. From this point there is a bus service that goes a long way round to Caernarvon, or you can make a very long traverse under the Elidirs to Bethesda. But for the evening stroll, make your way straight down from the Post Office making for an obvious track which traverses the side of a slate tip. At the end of this go down through the Allt Wen woods to reach the old Quarry Hospital and go back to Llanberis.

(h) Cwm Arddu

The valley through which the Afon Arddu runs is wide and long and rather dull, although it has good views of Snowdon on the way up. On one side the railway runs high up under a jagged skyline and, on the other, three minor cwms separate the scree of Moel Eilio and the crags under Foel Gron and Moel Cynghorion (10).

From the new houses near the Snowdon Railway Terminus, take the path to the waterfall, but soon leave it R to scramble up to a farm track near the top of the fall. Then a path by small farms soon leads to a cross track. Take this L towards a small cement transformer. Thence it is boggy to the shore of Llyn Dwythwch in the first of the side cwms.

For a short trip you can work up the R of the cwm to get on the shoulder of Eilio and return by a grass slope with wide prospect to Llanberis (10). Otherwise leave the lake R and swing round to the next cwm at any level desired to avoid the wet ground. In it you will find a track and a line of power poles that will take you through to Rhyd-ddu with the least rise, between Foel Goch and Cynghorion (10).

Unless traversing. you should not go far up this branch, but continue to the depths of the valley, above the waters of the river. Its upper part is called Cwm Brwynog and it is a long pull to the little lake, with a tail of tarns, that lies under the frowning cliffs of Clogwyn D'ur Arddu (3). After admiring the crags and watching the walkers and the train well up on the L there is nothing left but to wander back down the valley, with a good track to help from the farm, Hafotty Newydd, unless you climb up to Halfway House for refreshment.

(i) Derlwyn

Derlwyn (oak grove) (1,321), a little peak just above Llanberis on the Snowdon route, is a pleasant stroll, even if the oaks have gone. The way up is simple. Just go up the Snowdon Path and leave it L at the last cottage or thereabouts. The top can soon be reached on grass between small rocks. It gives a good all-round view, though the next peak cuts off the depths of the Pass. Going down to the col towards it, over a stiff wire fence, a sheltered steep grass slope L lands you back on the main road about half-way up Llyn Peris. By the way, as a variant of (2), the energetic should try a skyline ascent of Snowdon as far as Clogwyn Station, by keeping along the ridge, either from this hill or the next. The rise and fall is considerable, but the views are far better than those from the beaten track.

iii. CAPEL CURIG AND OGWEN

From both of these centres there are many minor excursions of interest and variety, since Capel Curig is on the edge of well-wooded country and Ogwen is near several cwms of much grandeur.

(a) Capel Curig to Llyn Crafnant

The walk to the lake, one of the best, is fully detailed in (21). When you have reached the lake and had tea on its charming banks, you can vary the return by wandering back among the rocky knobs of Clogwyn Mawr. There is also a jolly through walk down to Trefriw by the lakeside road, but it is not easy to get back from that small Spa.

Near the chapel on the lake, there is a path R that passes the end of Llyn Geirionydd, almost as big as Crafnant, and then splits into various tracks leading through woods that are dotted with tarns, either to the Vale of Conway or Betws-y-coed. By one of them the river can be crossed by the Miners' Bridge, below the Swallow Falls. But this is a long way from home, so take a sharp turn R, after a lake and near some old lead mines. A good track through some Forestry land will bring you down to Ty hyll, the ugly house. It belies its name, as it is built of rough stones and looks like a petrified log cabin. It is a good mile down stream from Capel Curig.

(b) North Slopes of Siabod

There are three river crossings in Capel Curig, the Cyfyng bridge, the wooden one at Cobden's and one behind Plas y Brenin. By crossing any of them you can wander beside the river and lake or rise through woods to higher land and get wider views. One of the best ways is to take the start of (19) and skirt the ridge above the woods. Then you have a happy time dodging boulders and damp spots and finally dropping down, by a farmhouse, to a fourth bridge at the west end of the twin lakes. The farm Duffryn Mymbr, on the far side of the road, was made famous in *I Bought a Mountain*.

(c) Capel Curig to Dolwyddelan

This is an easy moor and woodland walk on a well-marked path, often used by youth hostellers when changing their temporary homes. Pass over Cyfyng Bridge (19) and carry on for a quarter of a mile, turning R at a chapel up a steep hill. Open country is soon reached near the 1,000 ft. contour. Wide views to the south hold for over a mile and the descent to the Lledr Valley is through two woods.

(d) Capel Curig to Bethesda

This walk, mostly on the far side of the Afon Llugwy to the main road, is a pleasant level change from the ups and downs of most of the trips described. The route needs few notes. Cross the stream opposite the A.A. Box through an iron gate and follow the track for four miles, going quite straight after the early bend. At the farm Wern-gof-uchaf (19), regain the main road for a mile-and-a-half along the side of the lake to Ogwen Cottage. Turn in again by the Youth Hostel, for a pleasant continuation down stream for a good three miles and

In the Nant francon, Gallt yr Ogof on left,
Pen yr Ole Wen on right 7(iii)d - Photo E. Emyrs Jones

once more cross the river at the sixth milestone from Bangor, one mile above Bethesda.

In this second section there are bridges at Ty-gwyn farm and half-a-mile from the finish. These are sometimes useful for catching one of the occasional buses that run through Nant Ffrancon to Capel Curig. The only bridge in the first section is near the Climbers' Hut at Helyg, where daffodils bloom in the spring.

(e) The Miners Track

This double traverse from Ogwen to Pen-y-Gwryd is rather more than a stroll, but it gives as rugged a four miles as can be had without a peak, ending with a wide open view when you drop down on the south side of the Glyders. Details of the start are in (20) and the finish, in reverse, in (16). After passing Llyn Bochlwyd (1,806), you can pause by the low wall that marks the first col to note the next stage, swinging round the cwm to rise over the col on the other side. You get across to the worn path down some rough country, that is marked by cairns, not always helpful.

(f) Round Llyn Idwal

To circle this lake is a *sine qua non* for all visitors, not only for its own sake, but because it helps you to plan the major attacks on the fine peaks all round it. Therefore make the trip as soon as possible after your arrival. Starting just behind the car park at Ogwen Cottage the path runs up to the north end of the lake. Leaving it on the R, you pass the foot of Idwal Slabs, a nursery for rock climbers. After reaching the tail of the lake, you can inspect the Devil's Kitchen from below (17 and ii. f) and even go up the steep path to view it from above.

However, that scramble should be included in a longer day, and you circle R under the cliff below Y Garn, until you reach the tiny tarn, Llyn Clyd, right under its shapely cone. The brook from the tarn leads back to the larger lake and you can cross the main stream at the spot that you first reached it, to return by the outward path to Ogwen.

* * *

For shorter walks up the graceful slopes on the northern edge of our area and the charming strolls on both sides of the Conway Valley, you must consult local guide-books or ferret out your own routes, aided by the Ordnance Survey map. You will find ample choice, and it will take many visits to exhaust all the possibilities.

iv. INTERESTING TRAVERSES

From	To	Number of Excursions	Remarks
1. Beddgelert	Pennant Valley	7, 8, VII.i.d	Moderate
2. Beddgelert	Cwmystradllyn	7, VII.i.c	Moderate
3. Beddgelert	Blaenau Ffestiniog	15	Stiff
4. Llanberis	Rhyd-ddu	10, VII.ii.h	Moderate
5. Llanberis	Ogwen	17, VII.ii.f	Fairly Stiff
6. Llanberis	Bethesda	18, VII.ii.g	Moderate
7. Llanberis	Beddgelert	4, 6, VII.ii.e	Very Stiff
8. Capel Curig	Trefriw	21, VII.iii.a	Easy
9. Capel Curig	Dolgarrog	22, 23	Stiff
(Between Peaks	19 and 24)		
10. Ogwen	Pen-y-Gwryd	16, 20, VII.iii.e	Stiff
11. Bethesda	Aber	24	Easy
12. Llanfairfechan	Conway Valley	26	Moderate
13. Nant Gwynant	Dolwyddelan	15, VII.ii.d	Moderate
14. Nant Gwynant	Rhyd-ddu	4, VII.i.e	Fairly Stiff
15. Croesor	Blaenau Ffestiniog	14, 15	Moderate

The Idwal Slabs and Glyder Fawr, above Llyn Idwal 7(iii)f - Photo E. Emyrs Jones

CHAPTER EIGHT

A few Outliers

"The thrill of a mountain first seen or of a first climb attempted, remains for each newcomer a unique sensation."

G. WINTHROP YOUNG

WHILE there is plenty of sport on our own estate, a day or two in other coverts is always amusing. If there are any members of the party averse to strenuous exercise, they will welcome a motor ride to the starting point, which is always through delightful scenery. There they can hold the base while the ramblers ascend to the cairns. Notes on a few excursions outside Snowdonia are therefore given as a guide to such excursions.

i. Cader Idris

Cader Idris (2,927), well to the south, has a name learned in schooldays as one of the chief mountains in Wales and it is second only to Snowdon as a popular climb. It is a romantic peak in a grand setting. Whether it is approached by the steep north and south sides or up the comparatively easier slopes to the east and west it will furnish a good day.

Coming down from the north make for the road that runs from Ffestiniog or Maentwrog, by the side of the largest artificial lake in Wales, Trawsfynydd and pass down the wooded valley of Ganllwydd, where the Forestry Commission is doing good work. At its end, turn L for the old town of Dolgelley, over which rises part of your objective.

Dolgelley is an odd place; the houses seem to have been shaken out of a pepper-box, rather than arranged in streets. crossing the bridge into the town, bear R through it and as the town thins out, turn L off the main road, up a by-road that reaches Llyn Gwernan in about two miles. The lake is charming, with a hotel and parking place on its shore.

Nearly opposite the hotel, a fairly well marked footpath leads through rather rough country southward by a farm and then over a moor. It rises to a tarn L and then reaches the grim hollow in which Llyn Gader nestles right under the ridge of the mountain. Leaving the lake R you start up the famous Fox's Path. It is steep and not too clear, but its foot is marked by scree. The thousand foot climb is a bit of a grind, but not so bad as it looks from below. When you reach the ridge, turn R and reach the summit in three hundred yards.

The view is one of the widest in Wales. To the north is the Mawddach Estuary, with the Rhinog Range above. Beyond again Snowdon and its attendant peaks can be picked out. North-east, the Wnion Valley runs up to Bala, topped by the Arans and Arenigs, while in the east the low hills near Shrewsbury are visible. A stretch of the wilds of mid-Wales culminates in the flat uplands of Plynlimon down in the south. South-west is yet another hollow, the Dysynni Valley, ending in the Bird Rock that hides Aberdovery. Right under you on one side is the cwm you have climbed, while on the other is an even gloomier hollow, almost circular in extent, containing Llyn Cau, a lake that seldom reflects the sun.

There are four descents. You can circle round the amphitheatre containing Llyn Cau and find a steep way down to the larger Tal-y-llyn, but this will land you far to the south. East and west the skyline is tempting and both afford an easy path. Again the former, by which you can eventually get to Dolgelley, leaves you rather stranded, and to return by the Fox's Path is a bit of an anticlimax. You should try the western ridge. It is interesting and allows you to reach your base easily. Follow it for about one mile and then leave it R, where two upright stones mark the take-off. After that the route is plain sailing, roughly northwards. The road is reached at a farm, about half-a-mile beyond Llyn Gwernan, R. This way is called the Pony Path and an old guide book gave the price of a guide up it to the top as 6s., whereas the cost of a pony was 8s. It was not clear whether you could engage them separately, but horseflesh seems to have been more valuable than man power in those days.

ii. Rhinog Fawr

Rhinog Fawr (2,362) stands about midway between Snowdon and its rival, Cader Idris. It is the most conspicuous feature of the fine range of the Merioneth hills rising over the Irish Sea, as seen from the resorts on the shores of Cardigan Bay from Abersoch to Criccieth. It is not the highest of the half-dozen or so that top the 2,000 mark, but it stands out, a tilted cone, more clearly than the others.

The group is not easy of access, but is well worth an effort to visit as it always gives good sport. Run south again, taking the fascinating coast road that passes the round towers of Harlech Castle and on to the pretty river-fishing village of Llanbedr. Turn L before the bridge and go up the valley of the Artro for six miles, through shady woods and by a babbling stream.

The road, lately improved, is a bit narrow and quite busy

The Roman Steps 8(ii) - Photo R. B. Evans

in the high season, but with care you should reach Llyn Cwm-bychan near the foot of the miscalled Roman Steps. Miscalled because the experts agree that this unusual archæological feature is of much later date than that of the Roman occupation. The whole region round is full of traces of prehistoric man.

At the far end of the lake the car can be left by the lonely, ancient farmhouse that has housed the owners of the flocks and herds in this wild valley for 350 years. You will note that the rock of the hills all round is different to the volcanic and igneous stuff you are used to. It runs in flat layers reminiscent of the country near the Franco-Swiss frontier, between Besancon and Belfort. So rough is the going that the two historic paths that go through the hills are of great help to the rambler. One of these is the " Roman Steps " just ahead and the other the Drws-Ardudwy to the south, on the other side of Rhinog Fawr.

Even the mildest tripper would wish to see the Steps after getting so close to them, so you should wander across the bridge at the far end of the lake R and over a field or two. Then take any of the paths through the coppice beyond them and, on emerging from it, bear L over boggy ground till you find flat slabs, forming stepping stones over the bog. These are the first of the Steps. The path now ascends and passes through an impressive gorge. The steps are not continuous, but here and there a dozen or twenty stand together. The way is narrow and only men or mules could have used it, probably to carry ores and other goods through the defile. In a mile or so the crest is reached and the gorge opens out. The western prospect is wide, in direct contrast to the country behind. It is a dull three miles over to the hidden road that runs from Dolgelley to Ffestiniog (i). The far hills that make a fine horizon are Rhobell Fawr and the Arenigs. Before tackling the climb, a detour to the north to see the setting of Llyn Morwynion is well worth while.

The less active can now return down the Steps to the base, filling baskets with bilberries if in season, while the sturdy tackle some very rough going. P. Monkhouse, an expert, calls it "a grunt and a sweat all the way." Turn south from the track and work round a bluff and then scramble up a series of little cliffs, almost perpendicular in places. There are hollows masked by heather and bilberry bushes and a stiff sort of bog myrtle is also in evidence. From a stony plateau, you drop down to a pleasant little tarn, Llyn Du, and from its west end the going is better.

Half-an-hour should see you on the cairn of Rhinog Fawr, set in a stony waste. The view is novel and varied, with the greater part of Cardigan Bay to the west, far-off mountain masses to the north and south and desolate rolling moors to the east. The neighbouring heights look tempting and indeed they furnish some grand walks, but being so remote they are seldom visited except by Welsh shepherds.

To vary the return, take a line for another small lake, Gloyw Llyn, to the north-west. It is noted for large-headed fish that are always hungry. Leave this L and toil down one of the hollows bearing R till, at long last, the lower end of the Steps is reached. If you are a free lance, there is an easier way off the top, roughly south, to some farms in the next valley, Nant col. From Maes-y-garnedd, a historic manor house, there is a good farm track back to Llanbedr. You can reach Maes-y-garnedd by car if you turn R over a bridge, a mile inland from Llanbedr, and so tackle the hill from its easier side, but you will miss the Roman Steps.

iii. Manod, Nameless and Penamnen

In that excellent book *Afoot in North Wales*, P. Monkhouse says. "There is a hill called Manod Mawr on the far side of

Blaenau Ffestiniog, but it does not look worth climbing." For once the eye of this keen walker was at fault, for a very jolly day can be had thereabouts, in country that lies just outside the defined area of Snowdonia. Start from Manod Station at the south end of Blaenau Ffestiniog and take the secondary road just opposite the Station. This skirts the southern side of Manod Bach. Follow it by some cottages and then L into a lane leading to a farm R and keep by a stream L before the barn. A rough path helps and soon turns R to the corner of a field with a ladder over a high stone wall.

The hill is now reached before you, but carry on for a bit under it, till Llyn y Manod is reached. This lonely lake is between two hills. Your way is now up the boulder strewn slope R. It will prove neither as steep nor as stony as it looks; indeed, if you come across an old sheep fold near the lake, there are traces of a path through the boulders. Note the curious line of white quartz that runs up the hill, looking like a wall from a distance and the white splotches on many of the big stones. In under and hour you should reach the plateau that forms the crest, with a cairn or two that mark the way to the large round one, evidently the work of expert quarrymen, that is on the highest point (2,166).

On a clear day you will linger long in its shelter. Being on the other side of the Vale of Ffestiniog (14), there is a new angle on its beauty. At its end the sea opens out, with the white houses of Port Meiron over yellow sands. Further R is the pocket peak Moel y Gest, and the towers of Criccieth Castle on a seagirt mound. Southwards the waters of Llyn Trawsfynyd seem almost suspended in the air and, far away, the triple crown of Cader Idris (i) rears a ghostly barrier. Eastwards the wild lands of Migneint stretch for miles, the ultimate wall being the Arenigs (iv), looking very shapely and inviting. Nearer on that side is a compact cwm, with its inevitable llyn, with a line of cliffs called Graig Goch, more black than red, above the lake. The Snowdon Range make a brave show on the northern side. In fact ten of the fourteen three-thousanders can be picked out.

If content with this one peak, descents can be made from either side. By going east you can dodge the cliffs and bear R to follow the Afon Teigl all the way down to Ffestiniog, or by continuing a little along the crest, explore some old quarry workings L, threading your way through them and go either along the north shore of Llyn Manod or over the crest of Manod Bach to reach the starting point.

You will be well advised to pass along the skyline above

the old quarries, near a couple of tiny tarns, and over a defile with the odd title of Bwlch y Slates on the map. To reach the unnamed peak (2,158) you dodge some odd square chunks of rock. Here the full glory of the central giants opens out and Moel Siabod (19), showing its grimmest side, hides most of the Carneddau, but the highest can be seen, with the crest of Tryfan (20). An easy drop of 600 feet brings you down to two lakes, Bowydd and Newydd, that supply several quarries with water power. From their shores it is easy to use paths to get down to Blaenau Ffestiniog, but you should certainly carry on to an attractive peak, a little west of north.

After skirting the lakes by an old tramline there is a boggy mile to cross where you may flush a covey of grouse, though of late these birds are scarce. You end with an easy grass rise to Moel Penamnen (2,000) and stand silent like stout Cortez, except that the wide sweep before you is not a new ocean, but mainly old friends with new profiles.

And now, having done a good day's work, start for home. Come down carefully towards a small lake with a waist. Can anyone explain why so many mountain tarns are tight laced? The grass is steep and you will run, slide or " dot and carry one " till the bottom is reached. By the south side of the lake, along the boundary between Merioneth and Caernarvonshire, you can regain the main road at the top of the Crimea Pass and L soon be in Blaenau Ffestiniog. Otherwise follow an iron pipe near Afon Barlwyd and then by quarrymen's paths that land you in the main street of the town.

iv. Arenig Fawr

Down the Glaslyn Vale, from Aberglaslyn to the sea, there is a distant two-topped peak that bars the eastern horizon. Being well inland, it is the first to show the winter's snow and the last to be cleared in the spring. November seldom passes without putting powder on its wig. The peak is Arenig Fawr (2,800) near the wide open road from Ffestiniog to Bala.

From Llan-Ffestiniog drive up the steep hill past the railway station and on for eight miles over a fenceless road that rises to 1,507 feet before dropping a little to a place where the road, a single track railway and a stream, unite at Pont Rhyd-y-fen. At this point you're midway between your objective R, and Arenig Fach (2,500) L. Cross the stream and the railway and take any route you please up the grassy slopes. The way is obvious, but if you work L on the way up, you avoid the small cliffs that dot the rise.

Mastering the ridge, you once more find a wide plateau,

rising to the twin summits. From this, the most easterly cairn to be visited, you are well away from old friends and see a wide open vista in all directions. Only to the east can any cultivated land be seen—that running down to Bala. North and south unfamiliar hills stand in seemingly endless ranges, and to the west a wide defile opens out the far-off sea towards Portmadoc, with miles of moorland in the foreground. A memorial has been erected on the summit to the crew of a bomber who lost their lives near this inhospitable spot. Few monuments will be visible from such a wide area.

Sturdy free lances can have a pleasant walk eastwards to make Bala in about six miles, while real tigers going southwards can cross a series of fine hills right down to Rhobell Fawr (2,408) and reach Dolgelley in some 14 miles. Monkhouse describes this giant trip in *Afoot in North Wales.* The more modest with a car at the base, can either retrace their steps, varying the descent by keeping L off the plateau, or by going north-east to some cliffs and scrambling down them, near a brook, to the edge of Llyn Arenig-fawr, a circular lake in a fine setting. From either side of it there is fairly level going under some crags to the starting point.

v. The Clynnog Hills

Away to the south-west of Snowdonia there are two small hill masses visible from all the southern heights, adding variety to the prospects that contain them. The nearer is a square upland, with peaks at each corner, and the outer one, a perfect trident, as seen from the north. As both of them stand right over the waters of Caernarvon Bay, a profitable day can be had on either.

The Clynnog Hills make up the former group, Gyrn Goch (1,607), Gyrn Ddu (1,712), Moel Bron-y-Miod (1,365) and Bwlch Mawr (1,670). Owing to their position, they belie their modest altitude and appear quite lofty as you approach them.

To do this, you follow the southern coastline from Caernarvon to the village of Clynnog-fawr. Here is a fine cruciform church, recently carefully restored and well documented. It is worth a visit. This done, pass on down the road for a mile and park in the hamlet of Gyrngoch. On the L, behind a cottage, is a path that runs upwards beside a stream. It ends in an open hollow, and you turn R for an obvious way to the top of Gyrn Goch, a fine cone with a wide sea-view only halted by the west coast of Anglesey. Snowdonia stands out a solid mass to the north-east.

Passing southward along the top of the steeps that run

down to the shore, Gyrn Ddu is reached in about half-a-mile. It is the highest point of the group and the cairn is on one of those mounds of rocks, often found capping a grassy cone. Across a defile, the Eifls look well and, beyond, the land rises and falls into far Lleyn, while eastward you see a wide plain with Cardigan Bay at its far edge.

You turn south-west for the minor hill, Bron-y-Miod, just a heap of stones on a moor. Due east is a sharp little peak, with traces of prehistoric man, which is not far out of the way to the last peak, well over a mile away. This is stony round the summit, but you cross a wide marshy moor to attain it. A line of power poles across it is useful in misty weather. If you came by bus, you should drop down northwards to the upper farms of Clynnog. Otherwise it is easy to steer towards Gyrn Goch and regain the hollow from which you ascended.

vi. Yr Eifl

Down to the south from the Caernarvon road and from the Clynnog Hills, you saw and admired the perfect trident of Yr Eifl (1,849), rather well corrupted in English to The Rivals. As a last outlying excursion, they shall be visited. Passing on through Clynnog (v) and under Gyrn Goch and Gyrn Ddu, the road finds an unexpected gap behind the latter L, and climbs to the small village of Llanaelhaiarn, right under the objective. You can climb from here, but the way is rough and it is better to take a sharp turn R in the village, opposite the inn, and wind up round the hill amid the heather of a small pass. Park due south of the main peak where there is a by-road L (823).

Make your way across the moor to a small cliff and bear R to the outer crest. This is a noted region for bilberries and the bushes and heather make the going rough, but a little eased by paths and sheep tracks when they lead in the right direction. Near the first peak you will find Tre'r Ceiri (the home of the mighty), the best preserved prehistoric settlement in Wales. There are over a hundred circular stone dwellings arranged in rows with protecting walls. It will strike you that the long-departed users had rather less room than the occupiers of Council Houses today.

It is a slog over to the central and highest point, but from it you see a wide view that will include, on a clear day, the Great Orme, the Wicklow Hills and the coast of Pembrokeshire. The seaward peak is the top of a big granite quarry and has been eaten away for years. Steep narrow gauge inclines carry the stone to a small pier for shipment. Pass along near the sea when you leave it, to look down sheer cliff to a smaller quarry, Porth y Nant, also with a pier now disused. It is said that

Vortigern is buried in the cleft. Circling round the top you can descend to the shore by a path long thought too steep for wheeled vehicles, but discovered by motor-cycling fiends in pre-war days. On the heathery slopes up from the sea wild goats roam.

There are quarry paths over the moor to the base, whether you go down or not. All day the rolling hills of Lleyn have stood to the west and you may finish the day by driving towards them, through the village of Llithfaen, to Nevin. By the way, you have been following the old Saint's Road from the north to the Isle of Bardsey, where ten thousand saints are buried in a sea-girt cemetery. Nevin, too, now a trim seaside resort with two fine bays, has a long history. Edward I held a magnificent tournament here to celebrate the final conquest of Wales. Signposts will guide you back to Caernarvon, either through the busy market town of Pwllheli, the railhead and metropolis of Lleyn or, a more direct route, by a straight road east to Four Crosses and then L north. Both ways pass up to Llanaelhaiarn.

* * *

Dear reader, the tale is told, that last Welsh place name was tapped out with regret, since recalling those many days spent in the hills has given the same pleasure as was felt in tracing the routes. May you too find equal enjoyment, if and when you wander in this spacious playground. May the sun shine on your rambling.

APPENDIX I

The hazards

"Climb if you will, but remember that courage and strength are nought without prudence, and that a momentary negligence may destroy the happiness of a lifetime. (Do nothing in haste; look well to each step; and from the beginning think what may be the end.")

EDWARD WHYMPER

MAINLY owing to the far greater number of wanderers on the hills, the toll of accidents and deaths in Snowdonia has been increasing. The main causes are ignorance and recklessness. Hints at prevention (the better thing) appear in the text and these brief notes on cures may be of use.

Here is a sample case with obvious morals. At Eastertide, after a severe winter, the writer was on the Snowdon Ranger Path up Snowdon with an experienced climber. There was a good deal of snow about and some fine cornices had formed on the col above the Pyg Track. Just approaching this point, a young man in his shirt-sleeves ran over to us and said "My mate's stuck."

Going over to the edge we saw, some twenty feet below, a shivering lad who was unable to get up or down the cliff face to which he was clinging. It did not take long, aided by a rope from some passing climbers, to hoist him up to safety. He was chilled to the bone and, as there were no hot drinks at the closed summit hotel, he and his friend were sent down by their upward route, with a party that was going that way.

It appears that the young hopefuls had got very hot climbing up the Llanberis Pass in the morning sun and had left their cycles and coats at Pen-y-Pass to climb Snowdon, with its white peak shining against a blue sky. The path was mainly hidden under snow and they worked too far over to the left when they neared the crest of the ridge, with the result related.

These uplands are very spacious and it is not uncommon to meet people who are uncertain of their whereabouts. If the weather is clear, it is usually enough to point out the exact position on the map and indicate the best way to reach their destination. If, however, the meeting takes place in mist or in fading daylight or in any case where it seems doubtful if they can reach safety unaided, do not leave them until they are in a position to regain a path or highway by themselves. Company is appreciated when you are benighted.

There are rare occasions when persons, even of your own party, are overcome by exhaustion or sudden indisposition. Give the victim as much rest as daylight will allow, relieve him of any gear he may be carrying and encourage him to proceed slowly and by easy stages to a place where a conveyance can be obtained or proper shelter given, such as a farmhouse. Slow motion and a strong cup of tea often help to revive the over-weary.

The commonest physical accidents are sprains, bad bruises and broken limbs, resulting from a slip or severe fall. This is no place for a first aid treatise and the necessary treatments are pretty well known, but as sprained ankles are the most frequent casualties, it may be noted that the boot should not be removed, but laced tighter, and any available bandages wrapped over it and continued round the leg above the ankle, being tied as firmly as possible. The whole foot thus bound should be dipped in any stream or pool that is near. As a rule, slow progress can be made off the hill with the support of a stick or a friend on the injured side.

In more serious cases where the patient has to be left on the hillside while a rescue party is fetched, he should be made as comfortable as possible in a sheltered spot, with due regard to the danger of moving broken limbs. Every bit of spare clothing should be used to keep him warm and bracken or heather or even a low wall of stones piled round him to help keep him warm. If possible someone should remain with him while help is summoned, but in the case of a party of only two, the sound member must be sure that the victim will remain where he is while alone, even securing him with rope or belts, if he should be unconscious. Fatalities have happened where the injured one regained his senses and tried to move down by himself.

The recognised alpine distress signal, which is only to be used to attract attention in cases of *extreme necessity*, can be given by voice, whistle, handkerchief or torch. Six signals at ten second intervals are given in one minute, then one minute's complete silence, six signals in the third minute, followed by another silent minute and so on, as long as thought useful. The reply is similar, but with only three signals in one minute, and a silent minute between each of the three signals.

In the area there are Mountain Rescue Posts at Pen-y-Gwryd Hotel (Phone: Llanberis 211); Ogwen Cottage Outdoor Pursuits Centre (Phone: Bethesda 214); Hafod Meurig, Brynrefail (Phone: Llanberis 424); Aberglaslyn Hall (Phone: Beddgelert

233), spare equipment at Quellyn Arms, Rhyd Ddu (Phone: Beddgelert 267); Plas-y-Brenin, Capel Curig (Phone: 214). The Police can also be contacted at Llanberis, Bethesda and Beddgelert (Phone 222 in all cases). All rescues must be notified to the Police at Caernarvon (Phone: 3333). The R.A.F. Mountain Rescue Team, Valley, Holyhead, can only be called out through the police.

Devil's Kitchen, Cwm Idwal
E. Emrys Jones

APPENDIX II

Notes on the countryside

> **" The beauty and aloofness of high mountains and the hard physical effort which is required to visit them, combine to produce an emotion which has an inexpressible charm for those who have experienced it."**
>
> SPENCER CHAPMAN

DURING this century the town dweller has become acutely aware of the long neglected fact that he depends to a very great extent on the rural areas for his sustenance. Intelligent ramblers have always been interested in man's perpetual struggle with nature and its far-reaching effects. A few words on this point may help them, particularly as conditions in Snowdonia are different from those in the milder parts of this island.

Here are no waving cornfields or pleasant plains, but rough mountain pastures with a few green vales. Farming methods are, perforce, still primitive in the hills. Stock raising is the main source of the highland Welsh farmer's income. Sturdy black cattle, with samples of other breeds, are reared and sometimes sent to the lowlands for a final fattening. Dairy herds are not wanting, and milk flows, even if honey is scarce now. Lively mountain sheep are everywhere and the motorist should not be irritated with his prospective cutlets when they impede his progress. The clever dogs that control them are admired by all. A Welsh Sheepdog Trial is well worth watching.

There are one or two wool factories in the district. Good yarns and homespuns are produced but the bulk of the wool goes to Yorkshire and other parts of England. Horses are not so numerous now that the sound of the tractor is heard on the land. Formerly ponies and grand shires were bred and big horse fairs held in Llanrwst, Criccieth and other places. A few really wild ponies are still living on the Carneddau. The Welsh drovers who brought herds of cattle, horses and ponies on their hooves, right across England, are no longer a feature of Barnet Fair.

Oats, a little barley and potatoes, with some roots, are the only arable crops, and the hay harvest is usually light and late. These crops are mainly used to feed the local stock. As far as arable and pasture are concerned, most of the farms are small by English standards, but the uplands, mainly rough grass, heather, gorse and bracken, are of huge extent sometimes with common rights for the farms encircling them, but often with stiff boundary fences, that give the walker pause.

There is a grand spirit of co-operation amongst those working on the land, dating back to nomadic days, but also due to the shortage of labour and the heavy seasonal jobs, such as sheep dipping and shearing. At these times workers go in gangs from farm to farm to tackle the work unitedly. A "gathering" of mountain sheep is an impressive sight. If you come up in the winter, you will notice a great shrinkage in the mountain flocks. This is due to the practice of sending yearling ewes to the lowlands for grazing and to prevent them breeding till they are a year old.

Time works changes and one old Welsh tradition no longer holds good. It ran that, if you could in a single night build a house, roof it and have smoke coming out of the chimney next morning, you could claim the site and the land around it. Now many of the higher crofts are deserted and the upper hills are dotted with the ruins of former homesteads. Farms are tending to increase in size and to be cultivated by more modern methods, especially in the valleys. Agricultural colleges are doing good work and milk is now sent to a depot, instead of being churned at home. Today, Mr. and Mrs. Jones go to town in their own cars, often smart turn-outs, thanks to the kindly interest of the Government in agriculture. This also accounts for the improvement in housing and the rash of new wire fencing. Another novelty is the use of motor lorries to convey cattle and sheep from farm to farm or to the store sales that have replaced the markets and fairs to some extent.

The Forestry Commission is firmly established at Beddgelert and Capel Curig. In older days the vales and lower hills were covered with oak forests. It was said that you could pass right up Nant Gwynant on a white horse and only be seen at two points. Neglect and two wars have almost swept away the woods that hid Owain Glyndwr and his men, but here and there the valleys show how woodlands enhance the scenery.

In spite of the outcry about straight rows of conifers, the Commission's plans will benefit future generations, not only by helping industry, but by adding to the variety of the landscape. Even immediately it helps the visitor, since there is free access through the plantation paths, and surplus unplanted land, mostly in high and romantic places has been set aside as a National Forest Park open to the public. Here and there camping places have been provided, with water and other facilities for the camper and caravanner. Walkers will, of course, respect the warnings regarding the danger of fires in these areas.

The impact of the Industrial Age on Snowdonia is rather painfully in evidence. Vast slate and stone quarries fringe its edges, while waste heaps, trial workings and abandoned pits are found in many cwms. It is to be hoped that the C.E.G.B. will not further mar the beauty of this pocket Switzerland. Reference is made in Appendix III to some Societies that help to preserve the countryside and, now that National Parks are in being, there should not only be an end to vandalism, but some effort made to restore spoilt charms.

The antiquarian will find much of interest in the hills. In prehistoric times there was quite a population living in the high ground because the lowlands were undrained marshes. Traces of their settlements can be found, some of them quite well preserved. There are legends galore attached to the mountains and lakes and the study of place names is fascinating. The Romans came this far, and their roads can still be followed, even if they are not as straight as those on the plains. The heavy hand of the English conqueror is seen in the frowning castles that fringe the hills and coast. The Commandos who were lately trained round Snowdon followed in the exact footsteps of earlier warriors. Later, Roundhead and Cavalier measured swords in the valleys. Since then the tides of war have flowed elsewhere and for three centuries relative peace has reigned in these solitudes.

Finally it need scarcely be said that the neighbourhood is a paradise for naturalists. Geologists have an unrivalled variety of strata to examine; botanists can find an extensive flora and observe the effect of altitude on plant life; while bird watchers will see many old friends, and some new ones, in and around the hills.

SNOWDONIA NATIONAL PARK

No book dealing with activities in Snowdonia would be complete without reference to the Snowdonia National Park. The National Parks Commission have general responsibilities with regard to all National Parks in the country but the administration of the Snowdonia National Park is the responsibility of the Park Planning Committee of the Gwynedd County Council assisted and advised by the Snowdonia Park Joint Advisory Committee. The Park, which was designated in 1951, contains an area of over 800 square miles extending from the Dovey Estuary in the south to Conway in the North, and includes many well known beauty spots such as Sychnant Pass, Nant Ffrancon, Llanberis Pass, Gwynant, Aberglaslyn, Cader Idris, the Mawddach Estuary, Talyllan, Bala and Snowdon itself. The Park contains almost every kind of natural scenery; it has not only grand mountain ranges but also some of the finest woodland scenery and coastal landscapes showing cliffs and wide estuaries. An interesting feature of the Park is that the Welsh language is widely spoken, and the whole area is steeped with the influence of Welsh culture, literature and traditions.

The work and duties of the bodies responsible for the administration of the Park are summarised in this extract from the report on which the National Parks Act was based:

> "The broad objectives of planning in national parks will be the protection, and to a lesser degree the improvement of their landscape beauty, and the preservation of features of natural, architectural or historical interest, for the benefit and enjoyment of the nation."

As the Park is the home of a community of people, the Planning Authorities have a two-fold responsibility; on the one hand they have to preserve and improve where possible the natural beauty of the Park, and at the same time they have to consider the interests of the people whose homes are in the Park; these two things are not compatible with one another, and the Authorities are striving to preserve what they regard as their natural heritage and at the same time to ensure that the people are not bereft of modern amenities of life.

APPENDIX III

Countryside Societies, etc.

ALL hill walkers who take more than a very casual interest in the sport should pay the modest membership fees necessary to join one or more of the following Associations. This will keep you in touch with those that share your enthusiasm and you will receive much useful guidance. Even if you prefer to ramble in solitude, you should support movements that do much to preserve the countryside from threatened spoilation and provide facilities for those of moderate means.

1. THE RAMBLERS' ASSOCIATION

The Association functions at two levels, national and local. Besides arranging rambler's excursions, lectures and social meetings, issuing regular bulletins of news, hiring out maps and other activities, the Association performs valuable services in preserving the footpaths of our country, obtaining access to mountains and coast and generally in protecting countryside amenities.

Headquarters: 1/4 Crawford Mews, York Street, London, WIH 1PT (01-262 1477).

2. THE CAMPING CLUB

The Camping Club of Great Britain and Ireland is the oldest club of its kind in the world. Its objects are to maintain high standards of technique, to make known the advantages of camping and to protect the interests of campers. It has sections for mountaineers, canoeists and cyclists and special facilities for youth. Regional Councils and District Associations arrange local activities.

Headquarters: The Camping Club of Great Britain and Ireland Ltd., 11 Lower Grosvenor Place, London, S.W.1.

3. THE YOUTH HOSTELS' ASSOCIATION

The Y.H.A. is another practical society that does much to help the hill walker. It supplies the needs of country lovers whose pockets are not too deep. For a very moderate outlay, members are provided with a hot supper, bed, breakfast and a packed lunch, with reduced charges for those who do their own catering. It should be noted that members only are admitted and that advance booking is essential in the high season and at set holiday times. There are 14 Youth Hostels in the area covered by this guide.

Headquarters: Y.H.A., Trevelyan House, St. Albans, Herts.

Merseyside & North Wales Branch, 40 Hamilton Square, Birkenhead, Cheshire.

4. THE HOLIDAY FELLOWSHIP

The objects of the Holiday Fellowship are to provide for the healthy enjoyment of leisure; to encourage the love of the open air; to further the interests of education and culture; and to organise holiday making and other activities. There is a H.F. Guest House in Nantgwynant.

The Holiday Fellowship, 142 Great North Way, London N.W.4.

5. THE CENTRAL COUNCIL OF PHYSICAL RECREATION

In its work of promoting all forms of physical recreation, the C.C.P.R. co-operates with all the national Outdoor Activity Associations in the development of outdoor activities. The C.C.P.R. runs a wide range of residential courses at Plas-y-Brenin, Capel Curig, the National Mountaineering Centre. Further details from the Warden, Plas-y-Brenin, Capel Curig, via Betws-y-Coed.

6. THE NATIONAL TRUST

Founded in 1895 to promote the permanent preservation for the benefit of the nation of places of historic interest or natural beauty. In Snowdonia the Trust owns and protects much of the Carneddau and areas around Moel Hebog. The Trust is independent of the State and needs more members to support its work. Full details from the Secretary, 42 Queen Anne's Gate, London S.W.1. Area Agent: Mr. H. J. D. Tetley, Dinas, Betws-y-Coed.

7. THE COUNCIL FOR THE PRESERVATION OF RURAL WALES

This council also does good work in preserving our mountain heritage. It is in close touch with all the various authorities that have to do with planning and development of the countryside, in order to protect it from any threatened vandalism.

Headquarters: C.P.R.W., Meifod, Montgomeryshire. Local Branch: Mrs. Williams-Ellis, Ty Nanney, Tremadoc, Caernarvonshire.

VERB SAP

"The litter that one party of tourists selfishly leaves behind, destroys the pleasure of the next visitors."

G. M. TREVELYAN, O.M.